DIVIDEND INCOME PLUS

INVESTING IN THE STOCK MARKET SHOULDN'T BE DIFFICULT

RANJEET SINGH

Email: info@londonstoneinvestments.com

London Stone Investments
1 Royal Exchange
London
EC3V 3LL

Ordering Information:

Quantity sales. Special discounts are available on quantity purchases by corporations, associations, and others. For details, contact the publisher at the email address above.

Printed in the United Kingdom

Dividend Income Plus: Investing In The Stock Market Really Shouldn't Be Difficult / Ranjeet Singh.

First Edition

CONTENTS

PREFACE

I dedicate this book to my incredible mother.

Emigrating from Panjab in the early 1960s and marrying at a very young age with no education and very little money, she experienced some very difficult times. But that didn't stop her from dedicating an entire life to raising four children, and even two grandchildren after them. She selflessly sacrificed her own life so that so many others could live theirs.

Before my second birthday and in spite of barely speaking a word of English, my mother somehow found a way to teach me the alphabet at home. This was the moment that I fell in love with reading and writing.

I'm not a professional writer, much less an accomplished author, but I'm so grateful to have a passion for writing and this is all because of my mother.

In fact, all of my successes however big or small, I attribute to God and my mother.

A special thank you to my Mom, the most amazing woman in the world.

CHAPTER 1

A FATEFUL DAY

The date was September 15, 2008, and I was 34 years old.

I sat next to my grandmother on her small, tired sofa. My left arm was wrapped tightly around her far shoulder as I laughed. My grandmother was worried about me, she insisted that I had lost weight and that I needed to eat more. I hadn't lost any weight of course; in fact, I was several pounds heavier than I should have been. My mother smiled warmly at us both as she gently swayed back and forth in the wooden rocking chair across from us.

I wasn't particularly close to any of my grandparents who had all since passed, but there was something very special about my mother's mother. She was frail and elderly, in her 90s, but had an indomitable, fighting spirit. Born into abject poverty in Panjab, India, she often struggled to have enough food to eat, and so from an early age, she learned how to survive. Over the years I began to realise just how unique she really was, and it was inevitable that one day she would become one of the most important people in my life.

In fact, whenever I would leave the smog of London to visit my Mum in Coventry, we would never miss the opportunity to take the short trip to Birmingham to spend time with my grandmother. Just like my mother, she was a truly incredible woman.

So, there we were, sitting in my grandmother's tiny flat. In between joking, eating and reminiscing about days gone by, I turned my attention temporarily to the news on the television. The volume was muted and so I tried to make sense of the strange sight of people walking out of a skyscraper carrying overflowing cardboard boxes.

I looked more closely at the skyscraper and instantly recognised it. I had worked in the financial district of Canary Wharf in London for several years for a stockbroking firm and had walked past this building every day for many years. It belonged to Lehman Brothers.

The 150-year-old investment bank, one of the most powerful financial institutions in the world, had just filed for bankruptcy, making it the single biggest corporate bankruptcy in America's history. Those cardboard boxes were carrying the belongings of staff who had just been told that they had lost their jobs. My jaw dropped.

My grandmother and my Mum were still talking but I could no longer hear what they were saying. Time stopped as a thousand suffocating thoughts began to consume me.

SEVERAL MONTHS EARLIER

Several months prior to this life-changing moment, I'd quit my very well-paid job as a stockbroker with the intention of starting my own business. I had worked in the City of London since my mid-20s and as the arrogant new kid on the block, I had made more than my fair share of mistakes. For one reason or another, and almost always because of my distinct lack of maturity, I could never seem to hold down a job for longer than a few months.

Inadvertently I had managed to become an expert in the fine art of getting sacked wherever I went.

But at my last stockbroker firm, I was finally at a place where I knew that there was no risk of that happening. The boss loved me, the job was easy, and I was making more money than I had ever dreamed of. It wasn't a big company by any stretch of the imagination and yet I was making ten times as much money as I was making at Deutsche Bank – yes, ten times!

That's why the decision to leave and to set up on my own was a huge decision for me, a big gamble. I had been toying with the idea for a while but after my painful experiences of failure and rejection, I never had the courage to do anything about it. That was until my wife told me that I should believe in myself.

Although we fought like cats and dogs, I also knew that my (now ex-) wife talked a lot of sense and gave me some great advice. So, I followed her advice and decided to believe in myself. I resigned from my very comfortable post and dedicated my time to setting up the new business. I spent months completing countless application forms to gain approval from the financial regulatory body.

And now just as I was ready to turn my life around and begin my new business, the financial world collapses before my very eyes.

Without warning the very foundations supporting the global stock market had disintegrated. Suddenly everything that we had previously taken for granted including jobs, the economy, housing, cash, investments, pensions, was all at risk. The dark abyss into which the fall would continue and the impact that it would have on people's lives was unprecedented – it was unchartered territory for everybody.

Nobody knew it then, but the collapse was so severe that it was later officially recorded as the worst financial crisis since the Great Depression of the 1930s. It was and remains to this day the worst financial crash of our lifetime.

This was something that had been previously unimaginable. The scale of the damage to the global monetary system was unprecedented.

Ask anybody who worked in the City during that time and they will tell you the same thing. This was the beginning of the end. It was the economic equivalent of World War III. There was financial blood on the streets like never seen before.

What began with a crisis in the subprime mortgage arena in the United States, soon snowballed into a full collapse of the entire banking and financial system. People panicked as they ran to their banks forming queues a mile long trying desperately to withdraw their money only to be told that they couldn't.

As the world economy crumbled, so did I.

My whole future was jeopardised. I had just made the worst financial decision of my life. Everything that I had worked so hard for was now swept away in the middle of a financial Armageddon from which I had no escape and absolutely no control.

I turned away from the television screen and looked down at the envelope that I'd been clutching the entire time. I had brought it with me because I wanted to open it with my grandmother and mother so that they could give me their blessings. I wanted to share this special moment with them. Another mistake. After what I had just witnessed on television there was nothing to celebrate.

With my hand trembling, I ripped open the envelope. It was of course from the regulators, the Financial Services Authority (FCA), as it was known then.

This was it; my dream was about to come true after all these years. Except it had become a nightmare. What was supposed to be a joyous, celebratory moment was anything but.

Ten years earlier as a young, immature and arrogant University graduate, I had somehow found my way onto some of the most coveted and sought-after graduate training programmes in the country, including Lloyds Bank and the Royal Bank of Scotland. I even topped both of those by beating more than 5,000 applicants for one of the most prestigious graduate programmes of them all – to work for one of the biggest and best investment banks on the planet at that time, Deutsche Bank. I didn't realise it then, but I really had everything; I had all the help, all the training, the mentors, a great salary, one of the best work-placed pensions, the perfectly guided career path, everything that I could have possibly wanted. I was set for life.

And yet here I now found myself, alone and afraid. Just me, on my own. A stockbroker with no stock market to invest in.

I read the letter, which confirmed my application. 'Congratulations' it said, I was now officially the new owner of my own stockbroking firm.

Lehman Brothers, formerly known on Wall Street as '*Masters of the Universe*' had just collapsed in the worst financial crisis for more than a century and on the very same day that it died, and with some twisted form of perverted logic, I was now volunteering myself into the very same lion's den.

Where they had failed, I was now supposed to succeed.

I didn't know whether to laugh or cry.

THE CHANGING OF THE GUARD

Fast forward more than a decade, and I look back on that day at my grandmother's flat with inspired confidence. Whilst nobody knew it back then, that was the day that changed the financial world forever. It was the day that the public outcry was finally heard, and it was the day that financial regulators around the world began to make a difference.

It was the changing of the old guard with the new.

The fact that I no longer had the benefit of working for a multi-national company that earned billions of pounds each year, that had tens of thousands of employees, and that offered me an unrivalled level of support, in the end, turned out to be surprisingly irrelevant. Even though I was now working completely alone and had lost my support infrastructure, this had less impact on my journey than I had expected.

That's because there was a much bigger issue unfolding. The voice of the people was now resonating in the global markets. Although I didn't know it then, huge irreversible changes were about to take place that would change the financial markets forever. The business was going to change dramatically for everybody.

The financial regulators whose job it had been to police the banks, hedge funds, and other financial institutions were accused of being toothless and blamed for allowing those firms under their supervision to run the financial market like the Wild West. The Government was also heavily criticized and of course, that meant even more pressure on the regulators.

And that's what I mean by the changing of the guard. The regulations tightened dramatically, the whole rule book was ripped up and we were starting all over again. It meant that no stone was going to be left unturned, scapegoats would be needed and public hangings were high in demand.

As austerity kicked in and the general public began to feel the impact of severe cutbacks in everything from education and healthcare to social care and housing, the pressure intensified. The bankers were going to pay heavily for their greed; it was payback time and the regulators were ready to dish out the punishment in generously sized servings.

A new zero-tolerance approach to reckless behaviour was implemented immediately and compliance hoops just became a whole lot harder to jump through. Now the world had awakened to what really went on in the City and on Wall Street because the public was so fed up. It didn't matter who did the damage; we were all going to pay - including new firms like mine.

The excessive bonuses, greedy capitalist culture and reckless risk-taking were to blame for the crash in 2008 and even though this culture was in place long before I set up on my own, my firm was now caught in the crosshairs. The old game was over and there was a new game now – so firms either had to adapt and survive or they became obsolete.

In the end, things got so bad that the regulator even had to change its name from the Financial Services Authority (FSA) to the Financial Conduct Authority (FCA). That was an indirect admission that the FSA was not fit for purpose, that it had failed. The truth is that it was a politically motivated move to appease the public that real action was being taken.

It was the equivalent of the police losing control of society and the Army stepping in to restore law and order. That's what happened. New rules, restrictions, policies, procedures and a mountain of new compliance requirements came into force almost overnight and I was caught in the middle of the new political storm.

The new regulator wasted no time in making its name known. There was going to be a new sheriff in town.

I welcomed the changes being made because they tidied up the industry and I knew that eventually they would help to restore confidence. It would protect private investors from the reckless gambling strategies of big banks. However, I wasn't personally responsible for the sub-prime mortgage debacle, or the wagers that were being placed by multi-billion-pound investment firms, and yet it was the small firms that had to make the biggest changes. That's because we were running on limited budgets and resources. It took time, money and energy to create a business that worked in the new regulatory world and it wasn't overnight but took years.

And it's not even that the changes introduced were draconian or overtly difficult, they were just just different. As a new firm, I already had enough things to worry about and the regulatory changes just added huge new hurdles for me to overcome.

The extra layers of ever-tightening regulations made the difficult job of setting up a stockbroking company during a market crash even harder. I hadn't planned for this. I wasn't prepared for this. This wasn't written in the script that I had read.

Everything was changing, and my head was spinning.

The changing regulatory landscape also played straight into the fear of the consumer which meant it was even more difficult to win the trust of investors. Consumers were being regularly warned that the financial companies couldn't be trusted, the news was painting a picture that everybody who worked in finance was a crook and that people were better off keeping their cash out of the stock market, out of any assets. It was as if we were back in the 1960s and people were being told to hide money under their mattresses.

It's difficult enough to win clients from those more established businesses that have been around for years like Hargreaves Lansdowne, St. James's Place and other similar well-known names. These businesses have a trusted brand, an established reputation, and are viewed as much bigger, 'safer' institutions. They also have millions of pounds that they can throw at advertising, marketing, events and sponsorships to attract even more clients. And the added uncertainty and confusion that came during this unprecedented period of time made it so much more difficult to win business from those larger firms.

So, as a new business owner, I realised that I couldn't compete with the big players, I wasn't even anywhere close. For me it wasn't a case of competing, it was a case of just finding a way to survive.

SO HOW DID THE FIRM SURVIVE?

With everything that was going against the business, the question is 'how did the firm survive?'

Well, the market crash, for all the behemoth challenges that it presented, also came with a big positive. As the stock market prices were so low, it was relatively easy to make money because pretty much every stock that I recommended went up in price! And my ratio of winning to losing trades was off the chart, the best it had ever been – of course, that was the same for everybody else and not just for me. Everybody was making money. In fact, it's almost impossible *not* to make money when the market enters the first stage of recovery immediately following a severe crash.

Nobody knew it then, but it turns out that this recovery would be the beginning of the biggest and most impressive bull runs seen since the 1980s. For as severe and awful as the crash was, the recovery was just as sweet. The only problem was that in those early years start-ups like mine barely had any clients so couldn't really take full advantage of this move. That's why so many firms didn't survive and yet miraculously, with the help of God, things worked out okay for my firm. In fact, better than okay.

A rising stock market was helpful but it wasn't the reason why I managed to survive in the lion's den for as long as I did. After all, a new business can't survive on just a few lucky stock picks. A business needs a steady stream of new clients and it needs revenue – I had neither.

No, my success was linked to something far more fundamental than the pure luck of a stock market recovery. It was this same thing that helped me to navigate effectively through the new regulations, it was the same thing that helped me to win new clients, and it was the same thing that helped me to succeed when nearly every firm around me failed. It all came down to this one thing.

I know this because shortly after the stock market began to recover many new FCA-regulated firms sprouted up from nowhere. Some of these firms were even set up by former work colleagues of mine who wanted a piece of the bullish stock market pie as it recovered. Before you knew it, London was awash with small, independent firms like mine.

That's not surprising, because that's the way that market forces of supply and demand work. People saw an opportunity and jumped on the bandwagon. However, what might surprise you is that nearly every one of those firms failed. In some cases, firms lasted for a few months and in other cases for a few years, but in the end they almost all ended up folding.

You only have to look at the Companies House website or the FCA Register to see how many authorised firms either dissolved or had their licences revoked during that time.

That's why I know that if I survived and others failed it must be because I did something different to them – and of course I know what the difference was – it was my secret that I didn't dare disclose to anybody, a unique investment approach that I created. From the very beginning I tried not to follow but to lead. I did what I thought was best.

It was as simple as that. I had a different approach, a different plan, and thank God it worked.

I realised that I couldn't just do what everybody else was doing. I knew that there had to be a better way of investing, and if I could just find it, I would be successful. So that's what I did. I looked for a different investment strategy because I knew that the old ones being used couldn't work in the new market conditions.

The solution didn't come to me overnight; in fact, it took me many years and along the way I made more than my fair share of mistakes. I tried more strategies and investment approaches than I care to remember, and always in search of the same answer – to reach that holy grail of investing. To find that perfect equilibrium where my business could make money, and my clients could also make money from my financial expertise.

It was tempting to follow the old status quo but I knew that the traditional form of stockbroking and wealth management was dead. It would be just a matter of time before the world would wake up to that fact.

It turned out that I was right.

And, so for the first time, I am going to show you exactly what that solution was. I'm going to show you the investment strategy that I used and how it saved my business.

HELPFUL TIPS BUT NOT ADVICE

One final thing before we get going. For the purposes of full disclosure, the name of the FCA regulated stockbroking company that I founded in 2008 and still own today is 'London Stone Securities'. However, it's important to make clear that I am writing this book *independently* of the firm. Whilst the DIP strategy solved the firm's problem, this strategy really has nothing to do with the business and it has everything to do with me.

The firm just so happens to be the vehicle that I now use to implement the strategy, but I could implement it just as easily without the firm. In fact, I could implement it even *more* easily as I would have no regulatory restrictions.

That's where you have an advantage over me, you have no restrictions. And of course, you don't need a business, less still an FCA regulated business to use the DIP strategy.

This book should therefore not be construed as a financial promotion. Therefore, I need to make it clear that I'm not offering my services either as a regulated person or on behalf of my regulated firm.

I also would like to make it clear that I'm not offering any advice in this book either personally or in any professional capacity. I am writing this book from the perspective of somebody who happens to be a professional investor and is willing to share his knowledge. If you find my strategy useful and you want to use it then you do so with my blessing and if you don't want to use it, then that's absolutely fine too.

If you do use the strategy, then I wish you the best of luck and I really hope that you have great success. I would also love to hear how you get on so please keep me posted. It's the positive stories of the people that I have helped which really drive me to make my work public. I realise that my work is able to change the lives of so many people and that motivates me more than anything else.

I also have a website dedicated to this strategy www.dividendincomeplus.co.uk where you can get more free information. Finally, if you really want to take this strategy seriously and you want this to be more than just a casual read, there is an online course where I explain the DIP in much more detail.

So, that's it. I am not advocating, recommending, endorsing or advising that you follow this strategy. I'm just going to show you what I know.

If you do invest then you should only use money that you can afford to put at risk because there are no guarantees. There are always risks involved when it comes to investing and I'm sure you already know that things can go wrong.

CHAPTER 2

THE JOURNEY
TO YOUR SUCCESS

KEEP IT SIMPLE

One way to really understand the strategy is to keep it simple. I cannot stress enough the importance of doing so. Not only will I intentionally simplify things in this book to make the message clearer, but I encourage you also not to overcomplicate the information when you receive it. It's more powerful when you think of it as something easy to understand. Don't be fooled into thinking that it has to be difficult to make money, in fact, the opposite is true. Simple works.

Having a simple strategy to follow will also give you the confidence to implement it more effectively. If you complicate the system, it can become overbearing and you might just give up before you even start. If you keep it simple you will retain control throughout.

For some seasoned investors, trying to think of the financial markets as 'simple' may prove a challenge. That's because from a young age we are indoctrinated with the view that the financial market is complex.

However, the message of the stock market being intensely complex is a widely shared myth. It's used to convince retail investors that investments all carry the warning label of '*Don't try this at home*'.

That warning label is there only to justify the fees of professional advisors and make their position seem valuable.

Sure, you can complicate anything if you wish and certainly with the financial markets you can build it up into the most difficult and confusing thing imaginable. Inflation, interest rates, growth, employment, foreign exchange risks, political factors, company balance sheets, profit and loss accounts, price-earnings ratios, debt ratios, the list goes on and on. You can make it the most complex thing in the world if that was your intention. And usually, for the people who manage your investments, that *is* their intention.

That's because if you think that investing is complicated then you are far more likely to think '*It's far too difficult for me, I will leave it to the professionals to look after*'. And of course, that's great for your wealth manager, but not so good for you.

The stock market is simple. Making money is simple. There are just a few basic lessons that you need to follow and a few golden rules that should never be broken.

For that reason, I'm going to gloss over some of the technical aspects where I feel that it is necessary and make some simplifying assumptions if it helps me to get the message across more clearly.

This isn't meant to be a difficult, technical read. In fact, I want it to be the exact opposite. I want it to be simple, engaging and straightforward.

YOUR GAIN IS NOT MY LOSS

The stock market is big enough for everybody to make a profit. In fact, it could end world poverty overnight if it was shared out equally, which actually I believe would be a brilliant idea. Alas, I don't think that's going to happen. However, showing you the DIP strategy is my small way of evening things up a little for everybody.

The good news is that showing what I know won't affect me negatively at all. In other words, I don't lose if you win. If anything, it motivates me to help even more people because we can all win together. It gives me purpose and direction because ultimately what I want to do is to help people gain control over their finances. That's why I find it odd when people are so guarded with what they know.

If you know something that you think others can benefit from, then I believe that you have a duty to share it with the world. Everybody has a special gift, a nugget of priceless information, or just a useful tip that would help others – so why not share it and make the world a better place? You will feel good that you did.

And that's why I wrote this book, I believe that my small gift to the world is to help teach people what I know about money and how easy it is to make it grow.

I'm not pretending that I can teach you to become a superstar trader, but that's not my intention. My goal is to show everybody the basics of investing which will give them confidence and consistency in their results.

I also know that it's not just possible to make your money grow, but it's remarkably simple when you know how.

That's the thing about investing that most of the professional traders really don't want you to understand. They want you to think that investing is difficult and that there is a mysterious holy grail that can only be attained through a complex labyrinth of mathematical algorithms. But that's not true.

There is no holy grail and no complex path to wealth. Some professionals might try to sell you a formula to beat the stock market, but it's likely to be a lot of hot air.

Whatever the professionals might try and tell you about a special investment formula that is being used by some hot-shot fund manager to beat the stock market – don't believe them, it's all nonsense.

Those fund managers are taking risks, just like you are. And don't be under any illusion that what they have is infinitely better than what you have. Like in any industry there are a few elite players who are extra special but in the most part, the rest of them just have an FCA licence to their name and a very average trading background. That's the harsh truth.

That's especially true of the much larger companies. Think about it: if a company has hundreds of investment managers, they can't all be brilliant.

The truth is that there are many ways to make money in the stock market, and so there is not a single holy grail, but hundreds of them. You just need to find an investment approach that works for you and which makes intuitive sense.

LET'S BEGIN FROM THE BEGINNING

Should you decide to use the strategy that I am about to share with you, then you need to really understand how it works and how it came to be. Understanding the motivation and desire that was responsible for its creation, will help you put it in action. As they say, necessity is the mother of invention, and that was certainly true in this case. I needed this strategy in order for my business to survive.

So, with your permission, I am going to spend the necessary time to explain how the DIP was created from the beginning. In fact, the path to *how* it was created and *why* it was created is as important as understanding the strategy itself. For those of you who are keen just to jump to the more technical part and ignore what you might think of as 'fluff', be careful that you don't miss something that you might later regret.

It's one thing to understand an investment principle from a technical standpoint but it's a completely different thing to understand it from its *conceptual* perspective. In my opinion, understanding something conceptually is actually *more* important. And so that's what I would like you to focus on at this early stage because it will help you to make the right investment decisions long after you have finished with this book.

The question that you need to always consider is '*does the strategy make sense to me?*'

Even if you have no prior knowledge of investing, does it still make sense? If you believe in the concept and it makes sense to you, then you will implement it with confidence and have the best chance of success. Having a belief is an important factor when it comes to trading and investing.

Once you have a full appreciation for the strategy it will make sense to you in so many ways that you wouldn't have previously imagined. It will also be completely natural. And this is what makes it so powerful. When it clicks you will know straight away, and that won't happen if you just read the technical pages.

That's the lazy and ineffective way to investing – the short-term syndrome – the person who says, "just show me the system, let me copy it, I want the results and I want them now."

That approach always fails. Trust me, I'm living proof.

I suggest that you keep this book as a useful guide and read it regularly. The more you read it, the more that it will make sense. There will also be things which you will probably pick up on your second or third read which you missed the time before. Or you might see a different interpretation to something that I have written which will help you to apply it in a slightly different way.

I also encourage you to take notes, highlight passages, and earmark pages that you want to return to. If you are listening to the audiobook, stop and take notes whenever you need to. Be engaged with the strategy!

After over 25 years of trading in the stock market, and with what many would describe as having carved out in the City a successful career, this has certainly been my finest piece of work. I have tried complex strategies using options and derivatives, technical analysis and charting, fundamental analysis and balance sheets. I have traded the biggest companies on the planet to some of the tiniest, from the safest blue-chip shares to the most speculative penny stocks. I've traded shares and funds; I've traded in the short-term and invested in the long-term. I've traded foreign exchange, equities, derivatives and fixed income.

I've had many wins and more than my fair share of failures, but I have always started with the same objective, to make money, to beat the market, to find a better way. Each product, strategy and marketplace had its own set of challenges but the truth is that none of them gave me a clear route to financial success.

I have wasted many years of my life chasing the holy grail to only later find out that it never existed.

Don't make the same mistakes that I did.

The holy grail doesn't exist. **The DIP** does.

THE SECRET SAUCE DISCLAIMER

Now before we move onto the next chapter, let me tell you three things.

Firstly, in this book, I'm going to reveal for the very first time the exact approach that I've used and continue to use even today for me and my clients when investing. It has made me and my clients a lot of money over the years and I hope that it will do the same for you. However, remember that this is just a book and it can't tell you exactly how to implement the DIP any more than the Highway Code can teach you how to drive. You still need to fill in the numbers and build a formula. If you want to use mine, then I'm happy for you to do so but it's never a good idea to just blindly copy it. Therefore, I strongly advise that you use the information that I am going to share with you to build a framework which you can then use to implement your own formula.

This will help you to remain fluid and move with the market as underlying conditions change. You will see later on why this is important. If you do want to see my exact numbers and the formulae that I use, that's all disclosed in my course if you want to follow them. However, by the end of this book, you will have more than enough of a head start to create your own formula using your own numbers if you're willing to put in the work.

Secondly, in order for you to really value this strategy or any other strategy for that matter, you need to commit a reasonable amount of time and effort into it. That's the only way to appreciate its value because then you will feel that you have earned the right to get a return on your investment. Rome wasn't built in a day and if it was nobody would care about it. Anything of value takes time to build.

This book is not a get rich quick scheme, but it will help you to significantly reduce the time and effort that you would otherwise have had to invest yourself to get to this stage. It will take years off the time that you would typically need to spend learning but that doesn't mean that you should expect to become a master today. It's not easy to condense a decade of work, ideas, trades and strategies in just a few thousand words but that's exactly what I've attempted to do with this book. Now you need to decide how committed you are and what you want to do with these words to get the most out of them.

The impact that these words will have on your future financial success will depend entirely on whether you keep looking for a short cut or you are willing to put in the graft. Those who are prepared to focus their time and attention and are prepared to work hard despite the challenges, will get the most out of this book and ultimately give themselves the best chance of living a financially secure life. I'm living proof of that.

Thirdly, and whilst I'm not holding anything back in this book and will show you my strategy, I still can't guarantee that it will work for you. Nothing is guaranteed. Even though this strategy has proven to be successful for me and for my own clients, and has shown over time to be consistently profitable, that still could mean nothing to you. It all depends on how well you implement it. You may think that you have done everything correctly and for whatever reason, it still might not work for you. That's a risk that all investors take and if you're not prepared for that, then you shouldn't be investing.

Finally, there is one last point to mention.

Although I'm revealing my secret sauce principles, once you understand the DIP principle you are more than capable of creating your own. And don't worry if you think it won't be as good as mine. You're right – it won't be. It will be *better* than mine because **you built it for you**. This means that it will represent your investment objectives and your appetite for risk, not mine.

And remember that when the market conditions change, you should make changes to the system to ensure that it reflects those changes. That's why you should never depend on a static formula, the formula will change over time even if the principles won't.

Expect to work hard and make mistakes and by doing so, you will learn. This is just the start of the journey to climb the mountain and whilst I'm just showing you the quickest way to get up there, you still need to climb it.

The good news is that you have already started this journey by reading this book. Make a note of this now in case you forget - the end of this book is the *beginning* of your new journey, not the end of it.

CHAPTER 3

MY CONUNDRUM

THE GRASS ISN'T ALWAYS GREENER

Let's now talk about *why* the DIP was created. I'm going to take you through the exact same journey that I went through and at the end of it, you will see why the DIP became the solution to a huge puzzle that I had to find a solution to.

Let's go back to 2008. I had just left my very well-paid job at a stockbroking firm called Sigma Financial to set up my own stockbroking business. Even if I loved my job at Sigma and was very successful at it, I wanted to strike out on my own. Unfortunately for me, my freedom came at a big cost: I went from being financially secure to the uncertain roller coaster of an entrepreneur.

At the outset, I faced the same financial challenges that every other new business owner faces, and my goal was simply to make enough money to get through that first year until the firm was able to become self-sufficient.

However, setting up a stockbroking firm is notoriously expensive. I had fixed annual expenses that ran into several tens of thousands of pounds, in addition to the usual variable costs. And to top it all off, I was starting with nothing. No clients, and zero revenue. My cash burn rate was dangerously high, which meant that I had to turn things around quickly or I would become another bankruptcy statistic at a time where companies all around me were folding daily.

I had also made the decision that I would self-fund my business, rather than use venture capital, which put another burden on me. Having financial business partners would have meant that I had business experts to speak to and get advice from whenever I needed it, as well as an immediate support network and useful contacts. I didn't have any of those things. I had no help and I had never run a business before.

I just knew how to trade.

And as to my business plan, well that was another problem - I didn't even have one.

I just did what I thought was best – so my approach was basic, beyond basic even. No marketing plan, no competitor analysis, no financial forecasting, no cost-benefit calculations, no forward-looking business map, no projections or targets. I had none of those things.

I had a few people that I could call from previous companies that I had worked at to see if they would consider becoming my clients but that wasn't guaranteed to work, especially not in the current uncertain climate. Everybody had become insular and wanted to protect what they had, nobody was moving or changing their set up – I didn't blame them. Basically, I had to build everything from new and for the first time, I became acutely aware that the grass definitely wasn't greener on the other side. I was beginning to realise that I should have stayed at Sigma.

Now, here I was in my sad, tiny windowless office staring at a single screen with a telephone that never rang sitting next to it. I just did what I have always done - I hit the phone and made as many calls as I could. However, most of the people that I was speaking to had just lost half of their entire life savings in the stock market, and here I was, a complete stranger, trying to convince them to invest with me(!) They had no idea who I was, I had no track record, and my new start-up firm that I had just set up the previous week had one employee in it – me.

You can imagine the frosty reception that I received from them. Some of the shouted replies that bellowed down the telephone line consisted of two words and one of those was usually "off". I also remember hearing a lot of dialling tones as one telephone after another was slammed down in disgust.

That was hardly surprising. At that time Lehman Brothers and Northern Rock had folded, and a whole host of other companies were on the brink of going bust, including Merrill Lynch, AIG, Fannie Mae, HBOS, Royal Bank of Scotland and many other flagship institutions.

I was qualified as a stockbroker, but it felt at times that I was trying to do the work of a magician.

Even if people wanted to invest (and nobody did), you would have to be a particular type of risk-taker to want to invest with a company that had been around for two months, when businesses that had been around for a hundred years were going bust. And as every day, week and month passed, I was reaching into my savings and plunging further and further into the red. The pressure was on and the clock was ticking.

After much grovelling, I eventually secured my first few clients, but the problems were just beginning.

Now I had to find a way to keep these precious clients happy whilst still earning enough commission from them to survive. That was going to be another impossible task to overcome because I was faced with an excruciatingly difficult choice. Either I could adopt a higher risk frequency trading strategy, or I could trade more passively. This was my conundrum.

If I traded frequently this would generate more commission for the firm and if the trades were profitable, then it would also ensure more profit for the client. In other words, we would both win – the firm would generate enough revenue to survive and the clients would be happy as they saw their portfolios rise in value.

But this relied on ensuring that I would get most of my trades correct. I would have to average 80% or 90% rate in winning trades consistently and I knew that was almost impossible. I might achieve those kinds of numbers for a while and certainly, it would be more possible in a rising stock market but a stock market wouldn't just go up forever. Besides, nobody hits those kinds of numbers in the long term so this was a short-term fix only. It was a big gamble for me if I was going to accept that kind of bet.

I also had to consider that if I traded too frequently, in and out, aggressively buying and selling, repeatedly, this also exposed me to complaints and extra compliance risks because I had to ensure that such a strategy would be suitable to the profile of my clients.

And what if I got the trades wrong?

A quick succession of losing trades would be disastrous. If I didn't perform well for those small number of precious clients that barely trusted me in the first place, then I risked losing them completely and I would be back to square one. That would almost certainly spell the end of the business.

On the flip side, if I didn't back myself and trade aggressively enough, I wouldn't earn enough commission to keep the firm afloat, in which case I would be out of business in any case.

The clients didn't really care too much, either way, they just wanted to make money. No matter how aggressively I traded or how passively I invested – the important thing was that my trades made money. In fact, if my trades made money, then clients preferred that I traded *more* frequently, not less frequently.

But if I lost money then even one trade would be a trade too much.

So, you can see my predicament. Which business model should I follow – should I play it safe and trade infrequently, and only when I was highly convinced that the trade would be successful?

Or should I be more active and trade more frequently even if the odds were not quite so favourable?

When it comes to trading it's always about the odds and when to trade. No trade is 100% guaranteed so it's a case of just picking the trades that you feel will give you the best possible odds.

Ultimately that's why so many stockbroking firms failed at that time – and still fail today. They choose the wrong approach.

Many fell into the trap of trying to maximise their revenue and ignored the best interests of their clients. It didn't take long before they lost their clients and the firms disappeared. On the other side of the coin, the firms which didn't trade frequently enough failed to generate sufficient commission to cover their costs and also went out of business.

It was a precarious tightrope to navigate and very few firms succeeded. My firm was one of them and that's because I realised that neither of the two solutions on offer provided the answer which I was looking for. So, I had to find another solution that sat in between those two extremes – it couldn't be too passive and it couldn't be too aggressive.

So, let's look in more detail how stockbroker firms like mine make money and how the DIP strategy saved my bacon.

HOW STOCKBROKERS MAKE MONEY

It's important to understand how stockbroking and wealth management firms generate revenue because this ultimately determines the investment strategies and systems that those firms promote. It will also explain how the DIP strategy came about.

Firms are never going to promote strategies which don't make them money but equally, it's a very bad business decision to promote strategies which will only benefit the firm and not the end client. Finding the right balance between the two has always been something that many firms have struggled with and it's one of the reasons that most fail.

So, let's break it down in simple terms. Stockbroking firms can really make money in only one of two ways.

Either they charge a <u>percentage fee</u> on the total funds that they have under management or they charge a <u>commission for every trade</u> that they execute.

1. % OF FUNDS UNDER MANAGEMENT (FUM) MODEL

For the more established firms that already have a large number of clients, the percentage fee model works well. For example, if a firm has 100,000 clients and each client has a share portfolio which is worth £50,000 then the firm would have 'Funds Under Management' (FUM) of 100,000 x 50,000 = £5 billion.

If the firm charges a 2% annual management charge, then the firm makes revenue of 2% x £5 billion = £100million. (I'm making a lot of assumptions here but in basic terms, this is how it works).

The revenue of £100m is very impressive but this model obviously only works for big, long-standing businesses which have been around for many years, have 100,000 clients and funds under management that runs into billions of pounds.

But what happens if you don't have thousands of clients and you don't have billions under management?

What happens if you are just starting out as a new stockbroking firm and you have very few clients at all, and very little funds under management? That's exactly where many of my competitors and I were.

Well, here's the problem. It's impossible for any new start-up business to operate a percentage fee structure based on their FUM because 2% of very little, is, well, very little. In other words, all firms need to attract a certain number of clients in order to have enough funds under management to make an annual fee-based model viable. I call this the 'critical FUM mass'

Let me explain the Critical FUM Mass with some numbers.

<u>£1 Million Funds Under Management</u>

Let's say that a new start-up firm manages to get through the first few hard months and now has 20 clients (each client has a share portfolio worth £50,000), so the firm has funds under management of £1million.

2% of £1million = £20,000 revenue. That's not a business. That's a headache. With bills and expenses, the firm would be making a loss.

So, now let's be even more optimistic and assume that despite the difficulties of attracting clients to a start-up, the business has somehow managed to push through and has attracted a respectable 100 clients and now has £5million under management. To get 100 new signed up trading clients and £5m on the books is no mean feat and will probably take at least two to three years, and maybe much longer.

Therefore, and even after 2-3 years this still only equates to £100,000 (2% x £5m). This is a lot better than £20,000 but it's still not a sustainable business - remember that this is the *total revenue*.

The business still has to deduct its expenses, including employee salaries, office rent, telephone bills, regulatory fees, indemnity insurance, accountancy fees, trading costs, custodian fees, sales and marketing, corporation taxes and so on. This would mean that the company would almost certainly be operating either at or close to break-even. Once again, this isn't a sustainable business.

And what if the firm was only able to charge its clients 1% rather than 2%? This would mean a gross revenue of just £50,000. What if the firm could only get 50 clients? What if during that time some clients left the firm because they were unhappy with the service? What if some clients complained and won financial compensation from the firm for poor management? What if during that time the office rent increased, or employees stole client data and passed it to a competitor, or the marketing database became corrupted and you lost critical information? And so the list goes on...

You can see the sorts of challenges that start-up stockbroking firms face.

The point is that all start-up firms are a very long way off from reaching their critical mass and are faced with an upward battle. Therefore the Funds Under Management pricing method simply doesn't work for them. Instead, they have to operate on a *commission per trade* basis.

2. COMMISSION PER TRADE MODEL

A commission per trade model has pros and cons to the client.

One of the major benefits is that there are no upfront costs. Therefore the firm has to work for every trade rather than receiving a passive, annual income. This means that if the firm doesn't perform after say 3 months, the client can just cancel the arrangement and not attract any further fees. With the FUM pricing model, the annual fee is non-refundable and so the client can't walk away (without losing their fee) even if they are unhappy with the performance.

However, there is potentially one big problem with the commission-based model.

If we assume that a business charges a 1% annual fee on the FUM then this is the same if the business follows a Commission Per Trade model where the commission is 1% per trade and *one trade is executed for the full portfolio during the year*. In other words, the commission per trade model generates exactly the same revenue as the annual fee model if one transaction is executed.

Therefore, if the annual fee model won't work for a small start-up firm, then the commission per trade model won't work either. They generate the same amount of revenue if there is one transaction annually using all of the funds in the portfolio.

The only way for the firm to increase its commission is by *increasing* its number of transactions.

And now we potentially have a big problem because **a conflict of interest** has appeared.

The brokerage firm has an incentive to 'overtrade' for the sake of generating commission which will most likely mean that the client suffers. Instead of buying and holding investments for the long term which may be in the best interests of the client, the brokerage firm is keen to trade more frequently just to generate more commission.

But it doesn't stop there.

Most of the firms that started up at the same time as I did, chose this high-frequency strategy but they did it on turbo charge through *leverage.* This was all made possible by a product called *Contracts for Difference (CFD)* which was like share dealing but on class A drugs. Like the drug itself, it was a product that was badly abused by many stockbroker firms.

CONTRACTS FOR DIFFERENCE (CFD) & LEVERAGE

Leverage is where firms are able to take their modest FUM and multiply it – this means that everything is multiplied – the Funds Under Management are multiplied, the profits are multiplied (if the trades work) and the losses are multiplied (if the trades go wrong).

Most importantly for the firm is that the commissions are also multiplied.

A £50,000 account with leverage of 20 to 1 could be artificially inflated to become worth £1m! This means that the firm can now trade and earn commission on £1m instead of a measly £50,000.

Of course, this principle also extends to the firm's entire FUM. If a firm has FUM of say £5m, they could leverage i.e. multiply that by 20 to give a bogus FUM of £100m! Suddenly as if by magic, the firm can earn twenty times more commission than they could have previously.

The problem is that of the £100m, only £5m is genuine and £95m is made up of the clients **borrowing** money.

And borrowing £95m is great for the clients if the trades work but if they don't work, then the entire client account is at risk with just one bad trade. In fact, if a leveraged account lost just 5% of its value that would be the equivalent of the client's entire deposit being wiped out.

Of course, the firm takes none of the risk because it doesn't borrow anything.

Unsurprisingly, it didn't take long for trades to go wrong, for CFD accounts to quickly fall to zero and for clients to lose their entire portfolios. But that didn't matter for the CFD firms because of how much money was being made for them.

Thankfully I managed to avoid the whole CFD game because I was too busy working on a different investment plan but at the time

I remember that it wasn't easy to watch. It wasn't easy because I didn't know then what I know now.

I didn't know that those CFD firms were being unfair to their clients and that eventually they would all get shut down. All that I knew was that they were following a business plan and an investment strategy which was wildly more successful in generating revenue than mine.

MY COMPETITORS

Such was the amount of money being made by CFD firms that directors of those brokerage firms made millions of pounds whilst I was still barely out of the starting blocks.

Other than coming second at my kids' sports day in the Dads' race, I have never really ventured far into the world of professional athletics. However, I can only describe the feeling of watching my competitors get ahead of me as what an athlete must feel when he is constantly beaten despite running as fast as he can. After a while, it becomes very disheartening and it's not long before you begin to question your ability.

I would see these firms make huge strides ahead of my business, grow very quickly, build huge trading floors, make ridiculous amounts of revenue, post higher and higher profits and they were leaving me and my business behind in their tracks.

In some cases, specialist CFD firms would come into the market place several years after my business had been founded and they were still able to overtake me because their sole focus was on developing high-risk casino-style investment strategies.

It was as if my organic growth would take forever and there were many times where I questioned my whole judgement about the business. During this period, and whilst I was investing in research and analysis, my competitors were investing in Ferraris and Porsches.

The firms around me were expanding and recruiting scores of FCA-regulated advisors, salespeople, administration staff and building commanding structures to support their new business model.

They expanded recklessly and I was growing sensibly, even though I didn't really know that at the time.

CFD firms were all about size, leverage and scaling. It was about high turnover of clients and staff, hiring of large office spaces, recruiting and training dozens of 'openers' and then getting rid of them after a few months. Clients lost money and so came and went through a revolving door. That wasn't something to aspire to.

CFD firms became very big very quickly but with no substance. They just became inflated.

That was another thing that put me off, and that didn't sit well with my business plan.

I didn't care to be big just for the sake of being big. In fact, I already knew that biggest wasn't best.

I had already worked for some of the biggest investment banks in the world and as a young, impressionable man I was lured with what I saw at the time. However, my admiration soon disappeared when years later I saw one of my former employers, RBS, being bailed out by the Government. That feeling of disappointment was only deepened when my ex-boss, Sir Fred Goodwin, had rotten tomatoes thrown at the bedroom window of his mansion by angry pensioners who had lost their life savings due to his actions. I realised that the whole 'big is best' thing was just a farce.

The size of the organisation didn't matter, what mattered was the expertise and skill of the individual that was responsible for managing the client's investments. The individual fund manager, the investment specialist, the research analyst, the trader – these are the people that define the business. In fact, you could be a one-man band and still make your investors millions of pounds if you know what you're doing.

Warren Buffet is the greatest investor to have ever lived and his team today still only consists of a very small number of highly skilled people. In fact, I think I probably have more employees than he does.

My own corporate background, having worked for some of those big names, Lloyds Bank, RBS, and Deutsche Bank, gave me the perspective that I now had. It was by receiving my approval letter on the same day that Lehman Brothers went bust, which allowed me to confirm that perspective. I now really understood that the dreams that I had as a young kid to have a 'career' at one of the top investment banks was predicated on the wrong data. The bigger firms were no better than the smaller firms and just as prone to failure. In many ways, they were a lot worse.

This set me free because for the first time in my life I realised that I didn't want or need my business to become 'big'. In fact, I would go out of my way *not* to become big. Once again, the DIP strategy helped me to do this because it's a bespoke investment model which means that it's designed for the individual client. The DIP stops me from expanding recklessly. It keeps me focussed on what's important – delivering excellent customer value.

Building a larger organisation would have meant more time spent on recruiting, training, marketing and compliance and less time on what I knew I was good at – building investing strategies that could make money for me and my investors.

Because I knew that big wasn't best, I opted for quality over quantity. I recruited very selectively, and hand-trained those individuals myself. I grew slowly but with strength and stability and I invested more into research, analysis and development than sales and marketing. I spent more time developing my employees and less time on recruiting lots of staff motivated only by money which wouldn't fit into the firm's ethos.

So, I wasn't worried about size and expansion. I was worried about being left behind but I also knew that the Financial Conduct Authority would eventually become aware of the CFD scandal and shut those rogue firms down. It took some time, but eventually and after several years of watching, that's exactly what happened. The whole deck of cards collapsed.

CFDS ARE NOT TO BLAME

Despite the trail of devastation that some CFD firms left behind, I want to make clear that CFDs are not and never have been the problem. In fact, I have invested in CFDs for my own clients, albeit in a very small and controlled way, for many years without any issues. A CFD is like a spread-bet or an option or any other derivative -it's an investment vehicle. If used correctly it can be a very powerful tool (particularly in the hedging of a share portfolio to protect against a market crash) but if used for the wrong reasons (gambling) it can be devastating. That's what happened in the City of London for years.

CFDs were not to blame but the product still became public enemy number one.

CFDs just happened to be the perfect product within a perfect storm. It was open for abuse and the temptation for some start-ups was just too great to bear. All new businesses, including mine, faced the same challenge of trying to generate commission with a small amount of Funds Under Management.

That was the puzzle to be solved. And there were two approaches - one was the right way and the other was the CFD way.

The lure of earning ten or twenty times more revenue by switching from share dealing to CFD dealing was just too great for many firms.

The small number of firms that didn't go down the CFD route had to find an alternative and my firm was one of them. That's where the DIP came from. It was built out of necessity, not a choice. It emerged as my personal answer to CFDs.

And because it was built as an alternative to CFDs much of the DIP resembles CFDs in many ways; in all of the good traits that CFDs possessed. It was also through understanding the dangerous flaws inherent in CFDs that allowed me to design and build the DIP to avoid those same pitfalls.

I have nothing bad to say about CFDs. In fact, CFDs helped me because I realised that there was a lot of money to be made for me and my investors through the volatility of CFDs. It was the leverage that came with the CFDs that was unnecessary and amplified the risk. However, if I could harness and utilise the volatility of CFDs whilst simultaneously removing the leverage, then I knew that I would be onto something special. And that's what I did.

Ultimately this is what gives the power to the DIP. It has the risk of an equity but the potential of a derivative.

I am thankful to CFDs because it's a product which helped me build the DIP. The whole CFD scandal should never have happened but at the same time my competitors drove me to push myself and so in a weird way, I should be grateful to them too.

Without them, I don't think any of this would have been possible.

It was because I was trying to compete with them that made this whole thing happen. It fuelled my motivation to succeed.

I was looking for a strategy that could make money for my clients, that could generate revenue for my business, that could beat the stock market and to achieve all of this without the risks of leverage. I wanted a strategy that could do it all.

That's how I discovered the DIP.

CHAPTER 4

AVOID THE SHEEP MENTALITY

A WINNING MENTALITY

So now you understand the origins of the DIP let's move onto the next important step which is to understand the philosophy behind the strategy.

Trading is approximately 70% about mental toughness and psychology and only 30% about the actual technical factors. It's not really about the system, it's how you implement it.

Everything that you read in this chapter is about trading psychology and is an integral part of the learning journey. It will be key to your ultimate investment success. Knowing when to buy is one thing but being brave enough to do so when the market is crashing and everybody's telling you that you must be crazy, is another. That's why before you place a single trade you need to ensure that you have the right psychology.

In life, we all know that it's very easy and comforting to do whatever everybody else is doing. It makes us feel safe. However, that's not the right way to invest if you want to beat the stock market. That's why the DIP philosophy is very different from the philosophy followed by most fund managers. When fund managers construct investment portfolios, they usually have no interest to beat the market. Most fund managers don't want to beat the market, they only want to *match* the market – there's a big difference.

That's not to say that the DIP is either any more profitable or even better than any other strategy in the marketplace. That's not for me to say. Those who have invested using the DIP can make up their own minds and how they feel it compares to other strategies that they may have used.

But I can say this. I do know that the DIP does follow a very different **philosophy** to most.

I can also tell you that of the hundreds of different investment strategies that I have seen over the years, I don't know of any that have blown me away. In fact, I can't think of a single strategy that has consistently made profits without any losses. Not even mine.

They just don't exist.

The elite professional traders who have the best strategies all accept that even the very best trading systems can't always win. It's impossible.

That's why the best traders don't aim for perfection – they aim for consistency and reliability.

And you should avoid aiming for perfection too. I don't want perfection because I know that it's just a pipe dream. I just want something that I can rely on, that beats the stock market, that is profitable, and which works most of the time. That's the sensible game that I play and that's the one that you should also follow.

Perfection is not attainable and those who chase after it will always end up worse than those who aim for consistency.

There are also many strategies in which you can make money, in fact, there are almost an infinite number of ways that you can make money in the stock market if you understand it, so the secret is to find a philosophy that sits well with you.

You can think of the philosophy of a trading system as the roots of a big oak tree. The roots support a tree in the same way that the philosophy supports a trading system. Without a solid philosophy that you believe in, the trading system will fail. That's because when the system produces losing trades, which it will from time to time, it's the unwavering belief in the underlying philosophy that helps you to battle through and not become discouraged.

Without the right philosophy, you have nothing underpinning your ideas. The moment the system stops producing the results that you want, you will be quick to find faults that probably don't even exist, which means that you will change a perfectly good system unnecessarily.

The problem is that the philosophy for most of the professional market participants is the wrong one. It's just the way the game is set up. Big hedge funds and investment banks attract billions of pounds into their funds and are financially incentivised to be mediocre because investors don't hold them responsible.

The question is why don't clients hold firms responsible for poor or average performance?

SHOOTING FOR MEDIOCRITY

Manipulation is a very real thing in the financial world, and nothing is manipulated more than the expectations of clients. There's almost a full-blown conspiracy against the private investor.

Financial advisors, wealth management firms, fund managers, appointed representatives, account executives, salespeople – even down to the receptionist who answers the telephone. They all want one thing – that you don't leave their firm. They all get paid in some way from your fees.

They also know that the only reason that you might want to leave them is if your share portfolio is not performing as well as you think it could. But performance is subjective which means that it's open to interpretation.

I regularly speak to investors with the same risk profile who have entirely different expectations of what they deem to be 'good performance'. Some investors think that 2% growth per annum is great because it's more than their bank pays whilst others would be unhappy if they earned anything less than 20% a year.

And there lies the problem. Because it allows investment firms to manage, control and yes manipulate your expectations.

Remember that change is already perceived to be a painful thing and so it's not difficult to paint a picture that would discourage clients to move from one firm to another. They should stick with what they have and be happy.

Both the firm and the client hope that the investments will do well enough for the client not to have to leave. Of course, if the investments completely collapse, then clients usually have no choice, but it definitely isn't their first option. Clients don't want the headache of moving their portfolio from one broker to another, so they will find reasons to stay.

Change, doubt, inertia, worry, time, costs – these are all factors which stop clients from changing their brokerage firm and it prevents them from getting the best deal in the marketplace. It's the same with any other industry - once you are with a particular firm, you usually don't want to change.

That's what has led to this permanent state of mediocrity. The objective for most firms is all about 'just making enough' for the client so that they won't want to leave. It's not about performing well and certainly nothing to do with over-delivering.

That's why there are hundreds, if not thousands of funds which all perform very similar roles. There are thousands of investment advisors and fund managers who are all doing the same thing, just trying to stay as close to the underlying market as possible.

It's an overcrowded cattle market – nobody has any distinguishing features.

Of course, it's the safest place for them to be – huddled together. They don't want to risk potentially losing their clients by trying to create strategies which might offer above-average returns. Instead, they are happy to sit on the funds that they have and earn a passive annual income.

As a result, very few professional managers really push themselves and in my opinion, that's why the overall level of competence across the industry has fallen. The so-called experts are not learning new ideas or strategies, they don't need to. They are in a comfortable place so why upset the applecart, right?

The truth is that most financial 'professionals' have no idea how to beat the stock market, how to make consistent gains, or how to win more often than lose. It's not something that they have to do so it's not a skill that they have had to learn.

There is no incentive and no motivation to find a better way - this means that the financial industry (which is the most profitable industry in the world) is actually set up to *discourage* change and creativity. I can't think of any other industry that operates in this way.

A lack of creativity and change kills businesses in any other industry but in the financial markets industry it does the opposite – it allows businesses to keep an even tighter stranglehold on the Funds Under Management that they already have.

The only thing that will promote change is when investors begin to demand more from their financial advisors and investment managers. But the propaganda machine which perpetuates the myth that the stock market is this crazed, unpredictable beast that cannot be tamed persuades investors to stick with what they are told is best for them – investing in unit trusts, investment trusts, mutual funds, tracker funds. These passive funds barely move unless the market moves it for them.

It's the sheep mentality to investing and it kills innovation.

Worse still, it's sold as a low-risk approach. That's the problem. Investors assume that they are in safe hands but usually, they are not. They are with the rest of the retail investor herd which means that at some point they will all walk over the edge of that proverbial cliff together.

I accept that no strategy is going to work all of the time but at least when you try to beat the market you have a chance of doing so. When you sit back and let the market do the work for you then you *might* make money if the market rises but you are *guaranteed* to lose money when the market falls. That doesn't seem to be a sensible trade-off to me.

In my humble opinion, and perhaps I'm a little old-fashioned, all professionals have one job to perform if they are to be worthy of their title - they need to at least try to <u>beat the return of the underlying stock market</u>. That's it.

They may not beat it, but they need to *try,* and they need to do so without taking silly risks. And that's how I position myself, as somebody who tries to beat the market. That's my investment philosophy and I'm glad to say that I'm not alone – there are still a few of us around, we're just not in the majority.

There are professional traders on Wall Street, in the City of London, and indeed all over the world, who trade their own money or their firm's money. They are called proprietary traders. These are the people who I take my hat off to because they are innovative, they are creative, and they build strategies to try and beat the market.

They may not all be successful, but they all put their money on the line, and they don't just talk the talk, they walk the walk.

That's what I do. I invest my own money into the stock market too and I'm never afraid of following my own philosophy, my own trading system. This means that I don't have the luxury to sit back, be complacent and just let things happen to me.

But many professionals do exactly that.

It all comes down to fees and how firms are paid. Most fund managers don't get paid to make money; they get paid *not to lose* money.

None of this is illegal by the way, it's probably not even immoral depending on how you look at it.

If a client wants to pay a firm to invest their money into a few passive unit trusts and earn a return that's broadly in line with the stock market, that's their choice. If they want to pay a financial advisor another 1% per year for not doing a lot, once again that's their choice.

I'm not judging, I'm just telling you what happens.

And it doesn't matter whether the firms are small, medium or large – hedge funds, investment banks, wealth management firms, stockbrokers, financial advisors – they are all chasing revenue and commission. They just do it in different ways.

The larger firms are too inactive, and the smaller firms are too active. The former group doesn't do enough and just sits on their laurels collecting their passive fees, and the latter group does way too much and overtrades to make a commission.

That's not to say that I don't understand why earning revenue is important. We all have bills to pay and mouths to feed, and whether we like it or not, in order to survive we need to earn money. It doesn't matter if you work for somebody or if you have your own business, we still need to pay our bills. I totally get that.

I'm also not advocating living on a desert island and growing your own fruit and vegetables, (although admittedly that does sound quite appealing to me). I'm simply suggesting that many firms, certainly within the financial space that I operate in, seem to have lost sight of the very thing that caused the collapse in 2008 – not delivering value to clients. Before, it was not delivering value due to excessive, uninhibited, shameless, capitalist greed but now it's morphed into not delivering value because of chasing mediocrity.

THE RIGHT PHILOSOPHY

The smaller firms can't seem to cope with the burden of just trying to survive whilst the bigger firms are too comfortable to want to do anything different. Of course, there will always be firms like mine that don't fit into either of these moulds but finding them isn't easy.

They won't be the established branded names you would have heard of, they won't have the biggest marketing budgets, they won't be working with financial advisors who get paid huge trailing commissions to recommend them, and they may not even operate out of a recognised financial district, but instead choose to work from a small, remote office in the countryside. But these independent firms do exist and within them, you will find incredibly talented investment managers who are knowledgeable about the stock market. These are the firms and the professionals who I admire and respect.

The only thing that sets them apart from the others is that they have the right investment philosophy.

They share my passion that things can and should be done in a different way – and it's why they look at finance and trading with a different perspective.

It all comes back to the investment philosophy, and now that you understand mine, you will really begin to make sense of the DIP.

The DIP didn't just happen – it wasn't a coincidence.

If I shared the same philosophy of most of the other firms and my goal was to achieve 'average', the DIP would never have occurred. Without being able to truly believe that there is always a better way to do things, I couldn't have created the DIP.

It's the same for any form of innovation in any business, in any industry and in any country around the world. Like the great man, Mr Mandela once said, "*it always seems impossible until it's done*".

You must think differently, and you must be different. It's not easy to be a contrarian but that's what it takes to make money in the stock market because you are betting against the consensus. That's not an easy thing to do because it means that you are saying that the majority of investors are wrong and that you are right. Your investments need to do more than bob up and down with the market, those waves are for free. Those peaks and troughs are there for everybody to enjoy.

What you need to do is make more money during the peaks and lose less money during the troughs.

Only a different investment philosophy will allow you to capture more of the peaks and avoid more of the troughs. That's what a shift in mindset and a strong investment philosophy can do for you.

So, I would suggest that you now switch your own mindset into one of winning and not just coasting. Because to win you have to compete and you have to try. But you won't win by doing what everybody else is doing. It may seem like you are winning but it's a dangerous illusion.

Everybody makes money in the long term because that's what the stock market gives you, but you shouldn't confuse making an average of 7% per annum in the stock market as winning - that's not winning. That's just participating, and you don't need to pay a professional fund manager to do that for you. You can do that all by yourself, just buy an index rate tracker.

In fact, making 'some' money on an investment is the best way to mask an inefficient or risky investment strategy, because you're not losing any money. And if investors make money, very rarely do they question anything. They don't understand the risks that they are assuming for that small return. That's dangerous.

It's like swimming out into the sea and always finding your way back to the beach because the tide pushes you in. Even if you can't swim particularly well, and because you keep making it back to shore you became deluded into thinking that you're a great swimmer because you have never been in trouble before.

However, the one time that the tide goes out you are going to be in real trouble. That's when you realise that you really could never swim at all. And every few years when there is a market crash, that's what happens with the majority of retail investors. Some of those investors slowly make it back to shore but quite a few drown never to be seen again.

Most investors only make money because the stock market is going up, not realising that their strategy is flawed – either because it's inefficient or it's unnecessarily risky. But the rising valuation of their portfolio gives a false sense of security and paints an entirely different picture.

And when the stock market does crash, as it always does, the retail investor is none the wiser because everybody else around him has also lost money too. Therefore, the idea of making money and losing it as the market goes up and down becomes normalised.

The easy money is 'free access'. Without a formulated strategy that is measurable and designed to beat the market, you don't really have a strategy. You just have a collection of shares and funds.

This is all about the right mindset, adopting the correct investment philosophy and understanding the game.

Once you know the game, implementing the strategy becomes easy.

CHAPTER 5

DIVIDEND YIELD SUPPORT (DYS)

You have now seen my full journey and why the DIP strategy was created. You know the story and the history behind the strategy, you recognise the importance of the right philosophy and mindset, and you now fully appreciate the challenges that the strategy was designed to solve.

Please continually remind yourself of these learnings during your journey. They may play a more important role in you becoming a successful investor than the strategy itself. In fact, the investment strategy is the easy part. Any good strategy is mechanical, formulaic, objective, measurable and repeatable. You just need to punch in the numbers in the right order and then wait to collect your prize.

But your mindset and your emotions of fear and greed are subjective and belong only to you. They can be unpredictable which means that you can lose direction and hope. If you do find yourself in this position and it's quite likely that from time to time you will, then you can go back to the beginning of this book and read through these opening chapters. It will put you back on the right path.

If now you are in the right frame of mind and you are prepared to think outside of the box, then let's get down to the serious business of making some money.

It's time to dive into the technical and practical elements of the DIP.

3 RULES TO INVESTING

Investing is simple. Forget the complicated nonsense that you may have read about. Put away your book on Black-Scholes Pricing models and just remember these 3 simple rules:

Rule 1 – Protect your Investment

Rule 2 – Earn a regular Income

Rule 3 – Find Capital Appreciation

That's it. It's ridiculously simple and if you master these three things you can change the trajectory of your life forever. But if it's so easy then the question begs why isn't everybody doing it?

Well, I think it's because very rarely do investors combine all three elements together. They either focus on the capital protection and then make very little money because they are too risk-averse, they focus on income and don't make any sizeable returns, or they speculate looking for capital appreciation and end up losing big chunks of their portfolio.

There is no strategy and no cohesiveness of bringing the 3 individual steps together.

The other issue is that investors are being fed the wrong information. There is so much misinformation and noise in the marketplace, that investors are not making the right decisions.

Put the two together and you can see why most people don't make anywhere near as much money as they should.

When I was creating the DIP, this was my challenge. I knew that somehow, I had to combine these three elements together.

It was also important that the individual benefits of investment protection, income and capital appreciation were not diluted or lost in the strategy.

But what if it wasn't possible to bring all of the three elements together, which element could potentially be sacrificed? Which one was the least important?

I have always regarded capital preservation to be the single most important element of any investment strategy because it stops you from losing money, so I figured that this part had to stay.

At the same time, I also knew that income was integral to a successful portfolio because if the share price doesn't go up then you need income to give you a return.

But then, of course, capital appreciation was also key because that's what is going to give you the increase in asset value over time. Without capital appreciation, the overall returns would be minimal and in any case, buying a load of dividend-paying shares could hardly be described as a strategy.

In the end, it was clear that each of the three elements was equally important as each other.

In fact, the only reason that an investor might give a greater significance to one element over another is simply that it more closely matches their individual investment profile. In other words, if you are retired then you may wish to focus on investment protection, if you are on a limited income you probably want more dividends, and if you want to speculate you are going to be more interested in capital growth stocks.

And because I was building this system for my clients it meant that it had to flexible enough to suit them. I had to find one strategy which combined all three elements but had the flexibility to satisfy a broad range of investors, from income-seekers to high tax earners, from the young to the old, from the working to the retired, from low risk-takers to high-risk speculators.

The strategy didn't have to be a perfect fit for everybody, that would be impossible, but I knew that it had to work for the majority.

The strategy had to work for most people, most of the time and in most market conditions.

And at the same time, it also had to combine all 3 elements of protection, income and growth. To bring together all of those variables into a single strategy that made money wasn't going to be easy.

In fact, deep down I didn't even think that it would be possible.

It turns out that I couldn't have been more wrong.

PUTTING IT ALL TOGETHER

The problem with the 3 fundamental rules of investing is that they each work reasonably well enough on their own but when you put them together, they usually work terribly. There are compromises to be made.

For example, if you focus on rule 3 (capital appreciation) and you buy a high capital growth stock the chances are that it won't pay an income (rule 2 is compromised) and it's going to be high risk (rule 1 is compromised).

Similarly, if all that you do is think about protecting your capital (rule 1) then that's great to save you from losing money but it probably isn't going to make you very much profit (rule 3 is compromised).

And if you decide that income is your thing (rule 2) and if all that you know is how to buy good, dividend-paying companies, that's also not going to do much for you in terms of capital appreciation. Sure, you might collect some income but that's hardly going to set you financially free.

But then I started to play around and do some tests when I realised something:

Despite all three rules being very different from each other, there was a common denominator that brought all of them together. It wasn't obvious, to begin with, but eventually, I discovered that rule number 2, **earning an income** had the potential to bring all three rules together!

That's because rule 1 (capital protection) and rule 3 (capital appreciation) are diametrically opposed to each other. Rule 1 is all about trying not to take any risks at all whilst rule 3 is all about taking big risks to maximise returns. Therefore, I knew that these two rules couldn't work directly together.

In other words, through the process of elimination, rule 2 had to assume the role of the United Nations peacekeeper in this conflict.

If I had any chance bringing peace between the three warring factions and somehow getting them to work together, I had to focus on rule 2, the income.

And that's when I stumbled across my Eureka moment.

I suddenly noticed that whilst each of the rules sat in their own respective spaces (what I call bubbles), there was a small overlap between each of those bubbles. In other words, there was a small overlap between each of the rules where there was some commonality.

Think of the USA and Russia heading into nuclear war and the UK sat in the middle trying to negotiate peace. Whilst the USA and Russia have very different objectives, they also still share the joint objective of not wanting to destroy the world with nuclear bombs.

There may not be a lot of things that bind them together but the one thing that does is compelling! That's how I visualised the DIP working.

There was a small area of commonality, of overlap between each of the rules which helped to bind them together, which interlinked one to the other.

The mistake that I had been making up until this point was that I was focussing on each rule under the assumption that they were stand-alone elements.

After all, that's how risk assessments in our industry are performed for clients – they are individual questions in a very yes/no type format. We ask questions like: Are you a low, medium or high risk investor? Do you want income, capital growth or a balanced portfolio? Do you want a short, medium or long-term view? They are all very to the point and matter of fact – individual boxes are ticked.

This is what I had been trained to do for so many years and so I was conditioned into this way of thinking. I had never thought of combining them all together.

But once my eyes were opened to this, I saw that the rules shared more in common than what divided them. Wow! I would never have imagined that to be true.

And that's when I decided to push even harder.

Because I knew that there were elements where each rule overlapped with the other, I figured that I might be able to go one step further and find that small space where *all three rules overlapped*. I pictured a Venn diagram in my mind and it then all came together. When I stepped back and saw the diagram it made perfect sense.

It made more sense than any investment strategy that I had created before. Long before I worked in the City of London, and even before going to University, from the tender age of 17, I was constantly sat in front of computer screens trying to make sense of the stock market. More than twenty years later and I had come full circle.

This was the moment of two decades of work, imagination, creativity and luck. Everything that I had done before including the hundreds of strategies, the thousands of charts analysed, the trading screens that I devoured, the markets that I analysed, the technical indicators and the fundamentals, all of the courses and programmes that I attended, the years and years of learning, the victories and the losses, the ups and the downs – all of it right from that very first moment when I was just a kid and I decided that one day I would become a stockbroker – right the way up to now, it all came down to this one moment.

And in the end, it just came down to 3 simple circles.

Beautiful, isn't it? So simple and yet so powerful.

It's powerful because, in this small, confined region where each of the rules overlaps, there is a high level of concentration, where there is the greatest degree of synergy.

Those three investment rules each play a pivotal role in making money on their own, and it follows that taking the best bits out of each of them would make them work even better.

So that's what I did. I started to look at this area in more detail and played around with different ideas, different combinations, different numbers and variables. Eventually, my research led me to the discovery of an investment principle that forms the basis, the very foundation of the DIP.

Such was the impact of this discovery that I decided that it was even worthy of a name; I call it the Dividend Yield Support (DYS) principle.

The DYS is the mechanism with which the DIP operates.

The DYS is the operating system of the computer and without it the computer doesn't work.

CHAPTER 6

THE DIP SYSTEM

DIVIDEND YIELD SUPPORT (DYS)

The DYS is the bedrock of the DIP system because it answers that 64 million dollar question which is immortalised in the world of trading – "<u>when to buy and when to sell</u>". Technically, of course, they are two separate questions which are 1) *what price should I buy at?* and 2) *what price should I sell at?*

If you know the answer to these questions you basically become very rich.

And the DYS answers these questions beautifully without human emotion and with clinical precision based on mathematical logic. That was good for me because I have a maths background and I've always had an affinity for things which can be scientifically proven and make undeniable sense. The DYS does that.

Humans can lie but numbers can't. Either it works or it doesn't.

And trading operates in that way too. It's about numbers and probability. There is always a binary outcome – either you win or you lose, you can't draw. And if you win more often than you lose then you get rich and hopefully live the life that you want, and help as many people as you can along the way.

The DYS was like that – very black or white. It also uncovered something quite amazing.

It showed me that a dividend-paying share didn't just have the advantage of offering a passive income; it possessed a property which was far more important.

Yes, it was true that income was the main reason that investors buy dividend-paying shares. However, there was one other huge advantage to dividend-paying shares that I had completely missed, and it wasn't income!

This was the thing that changed everything and created the DIP strategy as we know it today.

I realised that the main advantage of income-paying shares bizarrely enough had nothing to do with income at all. The income, and specifically the dividend *yield* answers a far more important question which is nothing to do with income. You won't believe this but actually, it's to do with capital appreciation!

That's right, rule 2 (income) was less about rule 2 and more about rule 3 (capital appreciation). This was the part of the bubble where the two rules crossed over – the area of commonality.

Without looking, I had also stumbled across the answer to the two most important questions in the world of investing - 'when to buy' and 'when to sell'.

Think about this for a minute. Everybody thinks about <u>what price to</u> buy and <u>what price</u> to sell as rule 3, capital appreciation because it refers to the price. If you buy a share at 50p and sell at 60p then you make a 10p profit (or 20%). But the problem is that you don't know that you are supposed to buy at 50p and sell at 60p, right? That's the difficult part.

The whole 'secret' to investing is knowing when something is relatively cheap and when it's relatively expensive. For a hundred years, professional traders have come up with thousands of formulae, strategies, algorithms and techniques to predict what these two prices should be so they can profit from them. If you know something is cheap, you can buy, and when it becomes expensive, you can sell it.

If you do that often enough and with big enough size, it won't take long to become very wealthy.

And now here I was, and I had found out the answer to this fundamental question without even looking for it, almost purely by chance. That's right – I had discovered gold without even mining for it.

After some trial and error tweaks, I was amazed to discover that the DIP strategy could accurately predict, not always, but statistically more often than not, when to buy and when to sell.

This was the first and most important A-ha moment – there were several A-ha moments after this one as I worked through and refined the strategy, but this was the really big one. The game-changer.

HUMAN EMOTION AND PRICE

I had always known that the problem with looking at share prices is that it doesn't always tell the full picture. Prices change due to a myriad of factors including the company's balance sheet, earnings, profits, debt, corporate announcements, contract wins and losses, tax and regulatory changes, as well as entirely unpredictable external factors such as political events, terrorist attacks, wars and other unrelated events. Therefore, it's hard to value a company because there are too many unknowns and you're dealing with humans who can act erratically. Two people can take the same piece of news and act completely at odds with each other – one person thinks that the stock is overpriced and will sell but the other sees the news as positive and will buy.

That's why from when I was just a teenager when I first began trading, I have always favoured technical analysis over fundamental analysis because everything feeds into price action. Humans are unpredictable so rather than predicting what they might or might not do, technical analysis allows you to make money by just following the majority, even if they're wrong. The trick is to get out before the rest of the market catches up with them.

I know this sounds odd, but it works. If you have a room of 9 amateur investors and 1 professional investor and the 9 amateurs think that a company is undervalued but the professional investor knows that it's overvalued, guess what happens to the share price?

It goes up! Even though it shouldn't, the price goes up because the amateurs outweigh the professional 9 to 1, so even if they are wrong, they are right (at least for a while). Eventually of course the company can't support the unrealistic valuation and comes crashing down and that's when the professional is found out to be correct.

Therefore, in the short term prices fluctuate due to human emotion and are rarely accurate, but in the long term prices will always gravitate towards their true value. That's why Warren Buffet only invests in the long term and doesn't pay attention to short-term price fluctuations. It depends on which side of the coin you are looking at and how you want to make money – do you want to trade or invest?

Investing means going against the consensus which is difficult because your position will be 'off-side' i.e. losing money until the market realises that it's wrong and corrects itself.

Trading means going *with* the consensus even though you know that the consensus is wrong, and then making sure that you bail out *before* the market realises that it's wrong and corrects itself. That's difficult too!

You can see how psychology plays such a big part in the financial markets.

Think of it in super simple terms - if there are more buyers than sellers, then the price goes up. If there are more sellers than buyers, then the price goes down. That's it.

What it all comes down to is that a share price doesn't move up or down for any reason other than the actions of buyers and sellers. It doesn't matter about news flow or announcements – what matters is how investors *react* to that news flow.

And because different investors react differently to the same piece of news it's impossible to take any news and be able to deduce whether investors will react positively or negatively. Even if a company announces record profits, you will find that the marketplace has usually already anticipated this news and hence has factored it into the price *before* the announcement was made.

Therefore, when the announcement is made you can sometimes even see the price fall – it's the old *'buy on the rumour, sell on the fact'* strategy. That's why trading isn't easy because you are trying to predict human emotion which by definition is unpredictable.

However, there is one exception where human emotion is predictable and that's what I discovered with my strategy.

There is a universal rule which everybody follows which is quite simply this – if a company share (or any financial asset) pays a higher income than another company share, for the same amount of risk, people will favour the higher-yielding share. That's it – no ifs, buts or maybes.

If you give me a choice of either receiving 5% income or 10% income with the same level of risk, I'm going to choose the 10% income payer. There is no discussion to be had. And that's the same for every investor in the world.

PRICE IS DETERMINED BY INCOME YIELD

We know that income-seeking investors will only buy a share if it pays a dividend. It makes sense then that if all other things are equal an investor will be more likely to buy if the dividend is high and will be less likely to buy if the dividend is low. In other words, if an investor wants to buy a share and is choosing between two companies to invest in, and both are perceived to be exactly the same in terms of risk and potential capital return, then the investor will always choose the company which pays the higher dividend. That makes sense, right?

Therefore, it can be assumed that if the dividend yield rises, so will the buying interest.

For example, if there are 1000 investors who want to buy shares in company ABC when it is paying a dividend yield of say 4%, would it be fair to assume that there might be another 5,000 <u>new</u> investors who would be willing to buy if the dividend yield was to increase to 5%? And could it be possible that 10,000 new investors might want to buy the share if the yield went up even further, to say 6%?

And if the dividend yield goes up to 7% could that attract say another 20,000 new investors who want to buy that company? Yes of course.

Clearly, these are fictitious numbers, but it illustrates a simple point. As the income that a company pays becomes more attractive to investors i.e. as its dividend yield goes up, and if we assume that all other things remain equal, then it follows that more investors will want to buy. That's perfectly logical.

This means that as the income increases (i.e. the dividend yield increases) the buying interest also increases. Let's look at some numbers to see how it works in practice.

DYS NUMERICAL EXAMPLE

We know that when a share price falls in value, the dividend yield will increase. For example, let's say a company pays a dividend of 5 pence per share, and the share price is 100 pence; this means that the dividend yield is 5p/100p, which is 5%.

If the share price now suddenly falls to 80p, but the dividend of 5p remains the same, the dividend yield will increase to 5p/80p, which is 6.25%.

Provided that the company has not fundamentally changed and the risk has not altered, then any new investors who buy this share will receive a higher yield of 6.25%.

This means that new investors will buy exactly the same company in the same market conditions but at a 20% discount to what it was previously trading at (80p instead of 100p). In addition, they will also be rewarded with a 25% higher level of dividend income (they receive 6.25% compared to the previous group of investors who bought the shares at 100p and therefore received only 5%).

In other words, the new investors are better rewarded for taking on the same level of risk.

The discounted company share price plus the additional dividend yield is a big incentive and so will encourage more investors to buy this share. This results in more buying activity.

If the share price falls further this pushes up the dividend yield even higher which in turn attracts even more investors. Therefore, this means even more buying activity.

Eventually, there will come a point where the number of new buyers will exceed the number of sellers and it's at this point that the share price will stop falling and reverse. The downward trend will be broken, and the upward trend will establish itself.

So, then I asked myself another question - why doesn't the share price immediately go up when more buyers are entering the market?

In other words, when the share price falls from say 100p to 80p and the yield increases from 5% to 6.25%, and more investors start to buy, why doesn't the price go up then? Why does the price keep falling?

The only reason that the price can continue falling is that there are more sellers than buyers – but why should there be more sellers than buyers if we know that the company is offering a higher income yield? Why doesn't everybody just start buying? In fact, why is anybody selling?

This was my second A-ha moment.

THE TIPPING POINT

I began studying hundreds of different charts and looked at this phenomenon in great detail from an array of different angles because it didn't make sense to me. If an investor is willing to buy something at 100p and earn 5% why would another investor not be willing to buy the same company at 80p and earn 6.25%?

The answer was clear – it was about risk or more accurately it was about perceived risk.

As humans, we want to avoid pain at all costs. It's a survival instinct from millions of years of DNA which means that we would rather miss an opportunity to make money than to risk losing money in taking on an opportunity. So, when a share price falls, inexperienced investors will assume that there is something wrong with the company and that the risk is higher, even if it usually isn't. Similarly, if a company pays a dividend yield of 7% some investors automatically assume that it must be riskier than a company which pays a yield of 4%. Whilst that's true sometimes, it's not always true.

It's about perception and so one person's fear becomes another person's opportunity.

Therefore, when a company falls from 100p to 80p there will be many investors (already holding the shares) who panic and sell. They assume that the price must have gone down because the company is in trouble. This creates the liquidity needed for savvy investors who are buying. In fact, without the sellers, the DIP wouldn't work because the sellers ensure that the share price doesn't recover too quickly. Without the sellers, the price would recover from 80p to 100p in just a few minutes and the opportunity will have gone.

That's what happens with highly efficient markets and how arbitrage trading works; the smallest inefficiency is exploited which means that prices return very quickly to equilibrium, to what is regarded as 'fair value'.

But that doesn't happen here because of human emotions. And that's the opportunity for you to exploit.

If every investor knew what they were doing, you wouldn't have an opportunity to make any money. If I knew that I was only competing against Warren Buffet I would hand in my resignation tomorrow and learn a new profession. It's because the market is full of amateurs that allows me (and you) to make the kind of money that's possible. An almost infinite amount of money from an almost infinite number of people who have no clue. That's the harsh reality.

Most investors don't know what they're doing, which gives the opportunity for the small number of investors who do know what they're doing to make a lot of money in trading.

So, the reason that a share price keeps falling when it shouldn't is because of panic selling. Investors panic. It's not the only reason but it's one of the most important factors.

Of course, at some point, the only investors left holding the stock will be either professionals (who continued to buy the shares on the way down), private investors who didn't panic and realised that the share price will recover, and private investors who did panic but realised that they had missed their chance to sell and so decided to hold and see what happened.

Therefore, and for the first time, the number of buyers will exceed the number of sellers and almost as if by magic, the direction of the tide now shifts.

This is what I call the *DYS Tipping Point.*

And it's at this point that the pendulum will begin to swing the other way, and the price will increase. At the same time, the dividend yield will now start to reverse and fall in value. So now the reverse happens, and the price starts to rise, it reaches fair value but the momentum keeps it going, so the price goes beyond fair value until eventually it peaks and creates a mini asset-bubble. Then the sellers finally exceed the buyers and the whole pattern repeats itself. This pattern happens over and over again.

Incredibly the pendulum phenomenon answers the ultimate question of when to buy, and when to sell.

In fact, the DYS tipping point remarkably shows the exact top and bottom price. That's because when the dividend yield reaches the DYS tipping point, the price can be calculated.

Using this logic, we can now see that the share price of any company can only fall to a certain level beyond which the share price must recover.

For example, if we take an extreme example of the share price falling to 50p this means that the yield becomes 10% (because 5p/50p). At some point, the yield becomes just too irresistible to turn down.

If you could earn a 10% return per year from buying a share where you were confident that the underlying company was profitable, in good shape, was relatively low risk and had no plans to cut their dividend, then why wouldn't you buy? More to the point, why wouldn't other investors, investment banks and hedge funds buy? The answer is that they would, and they do.

This strategy is incredibly powerful but it's important that you can distinguish between companies which are falling for no reason and those which are falling for a good reason. You need to carefully consider why a company's stock price has fallen from 100p to 50p per share, because if the company has fallen on hard times and is expected to post poor earnings and so it might not be able to maintain its dividend, then of course that changes the whole deal. If a company's risk has substantially increased, then a new 50p valuation could well be the new fair price for the company, and a yield of 10% may well be at the right level to suitably compensate investors for assuming the new higher level of risk. These are the false flags to avoid.

That's why when I first began to set out what I thought should be the parameters for the DIP System, the most important thing that I focussed on was the risk. I was careful to identify low to medium risk companies where I could be confident that a fall in share price would be more likely due to poor decision-making by amateur investors rather than an increase in the risk of the underlying company.

In many cases, I found that the share price for dividend-paying companies would fall for no apparent reason, and fundamentally the underlying business had not changed which meant that the risk had not increased. I recognised that there was a huge investment opportunity to exploit if I was able to identify the false flags from the true buying opportunities.

GREATER THAN THE SUM OF ITS PARTS

It was important that I constantly referred back to the 3 fundamental rules of investment which are capital protection, income and growth. These 3 rules collectively formed the mystical equation which had to be cracked and when I applied my new-found strategy I was surprised to see how perfectly it fitted, as you will see yourself below.

1 Capital Protection – the best way to preserve capital is to do two things: a) buy low-risk investments and b) buy them at below fair market value. The correlation between buying low-risk investments and capital protection is obvious – as the risk of any investment falls the probability of not losing money on that investment increases. And because with this strategy, I was focussing only on dividend income paying shares which by definition house most of the lowest risk investments in the marketplace my strategy was immediately fulfilling the first rule of capital protection. I was also concentrating primarily on the largest companies in the market which again meant that I was investing only in low-risk investments.

The second point about buying below fair market value is important for capital protection because the ability for a stock to fall is greatly diminished if the entry price is discounted to the true market value. In other words, if a stock should be trading at say 300p and for whatever reason, you were able to pick it up at 270p you have already built in a 10% buffer. That's not to say that the share price can't fall further but it does mean that you have greater capital protection against comparable investments because you have already secured a sizeable discount. Because the DIP was all about buying as prices fall whilst risk remains constant, this meant that stocks bought at a discount i.e. Below Market Value (BMV) had more capital protection than stocks bought at a higher price. The same applies in reverse, buying a stock at a premium to fair value means less capital protection because they have further to fall.

2 Income – the DIP strategy is entirely 100% based on income and so this rule was easy to satisfy. However, because the income of the stock was greater than it would typically offer during other parts of the year, the strategy went beyond income in the traditional sense. This strategy would *maximise* income.

3 Capital Appreciation – rules 1 and 3 are very closely linked and it comes back to fair value again. If I buy a stock below market value at a sizeable discount, not only am I less likely to suffer a significant fall (high capital protection) but I'm also likely to experience a greater price movement upwards (high capital appreciation). Because the strategy was designed to identify undervalued opportunities across companies where risk remained constant, it meant that the potential headroom above the purchase price was greater. In other words, the stock had a high ceiling to trade into. One of the issues that restrict capital appreciation is buying a stock close to its trading highs. It's the equivalent of buying the most expensive house in the street – no matter how beautiful you make it, there is a ceiling price beyond which it is unlikely to breach. But if you buy a bargain on that street the potential for capital appreciation is significant.

And suddenly I saw a light bulb light up in my head – all three rules had been satisfied simultaneously!

This was the first time that I had seen this happen where all three rules had been fulfilled and yet I had been looking for this solution for years. The irony is that with the DIP I wasn't even focussed on these rules. It's as if it was because I wasn't looking for the solution to these 3 rules that I so easily stumbled across it. I was just playing around with income and dividend-paying stocks trying to make sense of price movement. I wasn't actually looking for the trading holy grail and here I was now on the cusp of something quite brilliant. The subconscious works in mysterious ways.

Hopefully, you can now see how this principle works. Of course, at this stage, I hadn't put any of it into practice and so it was just theory, but I was hugely excited by the prospect of trying it out with real money, more excited than I had been at any point in my financial career. If I had found the answer this would be a game-changer for me and for my investors.

It's incredibly simple but so, so powerful. Not only does it bring the three conflicting rules together in harmony, but it goes into granular detail about when to buy and when to sell. Not only does it explain why dividend-paying shares fluctuate but more importantly it tells you by *how much* the shares will fluctuate.

As somebody who has spent his entire working life looking at technical analysis and charts, this breakthrough blew my mind.

Maybe I've been living in a remote cave for the past 25 years, but I have never heard anybody else use or even describe this principal before and I have worked with many very talented professional traders. To be brutally frank, I still can't get my head around this today - even now I can't believe that I'm the only person to have figured out this simple system. I mean, think about it, what I have described in this chapter is not rocket science and yet if it can be proven to work in practice then it must surely be regarded as one of the most powerful investment tools at the disposal of any investor.

Perhaps I'm being naïve. Maybe there are hundreds of professional investors out there all doing the same thing and perhaps I'm the only one writing a book about it whilst the others are keeping it a closely guarded secret. I really don't know. What I do know is that I operate in the financial circle and I've never heard any firm or any individual trade in this way. No doubt after this book is released and if it gets enough traction there will be some unscrupulous people who might try to put their name to it. But that's not my concern.

As I said before the DIP is there for everybody to enjoy and use no matter how precious it is to me personally.

Either way, what a game-changer it became for me and my investors over the years.

Whereas before I had to look at support and resistance levels, and technical indicators including moving averages, stochastics, candlesticks, volumes, and a lot of other hocus-pocus, now I just needed to know the dividend yield. Life just becomes a whole lot easier.

Of course, there is a lot more to this strategy in terms of implementation, which I will show you, but in this short description, you've now seen the foundation of the whole strategy. It's all based on the dividend yield.

Take a little break and re-read this chapter again for good measure before you move on. I want you to really appreciate the simplicity and power of the words that you have just read. I promise you that this is financial trading at its most powerful.

And don't be fooled by how easy it is – yes, it is easy and that's what makes it so powerful. However, you still need to know how to implement it correctly.

THE DIP WHEEL

The DIP can be broken down into 5 distinct steps which I refer to as spokes. When you put the spokes together you have the entire system, which is the DIP Wheel. I thought that this was a particularly apt name because the wheel must be one of the simplest inventions in the world and yet one which has had the most profound impact.

I also built the system in a way that makes the most intuitive sense to me so that I could implement it easily. I have had this obsession of simplifying concepts to make them intuitively easier to understand, ever since my University days. That was because I was spending too much time enjoying myself and not enough time studying and so I had to find a way to grasp and memorise information quickly. This approach helped me then and so I guess I have carried it out throughout my life ever since. And that's how the DIP wheel was created – simplicity often equals power.

Each spoke is simple but important because it performs a specific purpose.

Let's now go through each of the 5 spokes, starting off with the first one which in fact is the most important of all, assessing the risk.

CHAPTER 7

SPOKE 1 - WHAT'S THE RISK?

Unsurprisingly we start off with the most important factor of all, risk.

The first spoke of the DIP Wheel is therefore to identify the companies to invest in by measuring their risk. Remember that we only want to look at low-medium risk companies so that we can side-step as many of those false flags as possible. We won't miss them all and invariably one might get lured by the odd one or two but having a strong initial risk assessment enables us to keep those flags to a minimum.

The question is how to measure risk because there are lots of different ways, and through my research, I have found some to be more effective than others. Through different testing, I settled on another simple but efficient formula which I now use, and I have found that it allows me to maintain consistency in my approach.

What I am showing here is the final and most polished version of all of my work. Over the years, I have tested a wide range of different risk variables and I have analysed the results in detail. Remember that with trading you can't get perfection because it doesn't exist and so it's all about tipping the balance of probability into your favour. That's the secret to trading.

I also recognised that some compromises were necessary depending on which variables I used. For example, if I wanted to reduce risk in one area of a company, I might find that could potentially increase risk in another area. Admittedly, that was a bit of a challenge.

In the end, I finally worked through a labyrinth of different options and settled on five risk variables where I felt that the overall risk was least prevalent. I also managed to find a combination where the risk factors that I chose helped to complement each other rather than compromise each other.

To further accentuate the point I assigned a 'weighting of importance' to each risk variable with regards to how important I believed it to be.

Remember that you can approach risk through a range of different approaches. You can look at it through different lenses.

But the one thing that does not vary is the foundation that the risk spoke not only sets the tone for the rest of the strategy but is also the most important.

In line with following my preferred approach of a simplified methodology, I developed a 'traffic light' system of low, medium and high risk. This enabled me to take complex variables (risk) and convert them into basic pictorial form.

An unfortunate complication with risk which I was unable to avoid and despite my best efforts, is that it operates from a multi-dimensional plane. The company risk works in a 2-dimensional linear fashion and is relatively easy to calculate, but it sits on top of another layer of risk which is the overall market risk i.e. the global economic situation, domestic interest rates, taxation, regulation, political uncertainty and so on.

And market risk also has an impact on the DIP calculation because when assessing the risk of a company the underlying market conditions cannot be ignored. If the stock market is looking shaky and possibly showing signs of a market correction, your risk analysis needs to reflect this. You need to quickly tighten up your risk criteria which ensures that only the safest companies pass the test.

Remember that the best strategies allow for flexibility.

You may have a great sailing boat but if you're sailing into very choppy waters with a hurricane storm ahead of you, then you need to make the necessary adjustments. That's the same with the market. If the world is heading into a global recession, then even the best companies are going to suffer. That's what this whole game is about. Being flexible and sensitive to your environment.

The more you understand the risk the better you can understand how to manage and navigate round it which in turn improves your success ratio of winning trades.

So, what's the biggest risk?

Well, at the company level the biggest risk is if the company scraps its dividend. That's why each of the five risk variables all fundamentally share one common denominator – what is the risk of a dividend cut?

After all, this is the biggest risk to the whole system. If a company cuts its dividend then the whole system fails. It's the equivalent of the boat capsizing.

Without the dividends from the shares, there is no income, and without income, there is no DIP. It's really as simple as that. The next question is how do we mitigate that risk?

5 PILLARS OF RISK ASSESSMENT

RISK 1 - DIVIDEND COVER

The dividend cover is a measure of the company's ability to pay its dividend. For example, if a company has a dividend cover of 2, this suggests that the company can pay its dividend twice over. In other words, it is generating enough profit to comfortably pay its shareholders.

Therefore, a share with a low dividend cover suggests that the company is paying out a disproportionately large percentage of its earnings as dividends. That's not good news because it means that the company might be paying a decent dividend now but is pushing beyond its means.

Think of it like somebody overspending on their credit card each month and only just about keeping up with their payments. If they have one bad month they might struggle and might have less cash to cover their next payment. Worse still, if things don't improve, they could even default on the whole debt.

That's why for the DIP strategy the dividend cover is one of the single most important factors in establishing risk. After all, this entire strategy is predicated on the dividend and the biggest risk factor for this strategy not to work is for the company to cut its dividend. In other words, the strategy only works if the company continues to honour the dividends that it was expected to pay.

If it doesn't do that, then we could be in a whole world of trouble because a dividend cut not only impacts the income but more importantly it will have a detrimental impact on the share price. More about this later, but for now just be very conscious of the dividend cover.

RISK 2 - SIZE OF COMPANY (MARKET CAPITALISATION)

The second element of risk to consider is the size of the company. The assumption here is that the bigger the company, the lower the risk. Whilst this doesn't mean that big companies can't crumble, it does usually give investors greater protection than less established or smaller companies.

For example, if you are a low-risk investor you may wish to focus only on the largest companies in the stock market. In the UK, which is the market that I tend to invest in most, the largest (and therefore lowest risk) shares are found in the FTSE100 index. The next tier down is the FTSE250 index which houses the UK's next largest 250 companies, and if you are a higher-risk investor you could even stretch this strategy out to smaller companies which are on the Alternative Investment Market (AIM).

If a company is of a certain size, it will have a presence and reputation in the marketplace which it will want to protect. This means that the bigger companies are likely to continue to pay dividends on their stocks, even when things get a little rocky. They also typically have larger cash reserves and retained earnings from previous years and will therefore usually be able to weather the storm if things get rough for a while. Furthermore, you usually get a lot of warning ahead of any action being taken because the big names see a dividend cut as a major defeat and it's viewed as a last resort option.

Unfortunately, smaller companies don't have that same luxury. When faced with financial difficulty, one of the first non-essential expenses that a small AIM company might consider cutting is the dividend.

I personally focus almost exclusively on the FTSE 350 companies (FTSE 100 & 250) companies because it matches my clients' risk appetite more closely, but I have had good results in the AIM market also. The important point here is to choose a market and stick to it, at least at the start. Be very wary about 'chopping and changing' your system, especially very early on, because you are likely to chase the market for the results which can be damaging. Don't chase the market, be patient and let the opportunities come to you.

Of course, it's not always the case that big firms are low risk and that small firms are high risk, but as a general rule, it's a sensible position to assume as part of your wider assessment of risk.

RISK 3 - FREE CASHFLOW

The 'free' cashflow of a company is the third indicator that I use to establish risk. That's because cash is critical to pay dividends. It also shows you the ability of the company to repay its debt obligations including interest on loans. Often, I see investors look at the profit of a business in isolation, which is a mistake as profits only tell you half of the picture.

The old adage of 'cash is king' is absolutely true when it comes to measuring the risk of a company. A high cashflow number on its own however could be misleading because cash can be generated in any number of ways, including selling off business assets or taking on extra debt. This is not the kind of cash flow that I'm interested in.

That's the reason I favour *free* cash flow because this is the real amount of cash that's left in the business after all the bills have been paid. In other words, it's a more stringent measure of what's left in the coffers after interest, capital expenditure and dividends have been paid.

And yes, you guessed it, the better the free cash flow number, the less chance I am going to be worried that the company is going to cut its dividend any time soon.

RISK 4 - MANAGEMENT

There is no getting away from the management team because the directors are the captains of the proverbial ship. If they make the right decisions the ship sails into the sunset but if they get it wrong, it hits an iceberg and sinks. That's why I like to see stability and longevity in the management team.

You might want to ask questions such as: How long has the management team been working at that company? How often does senior management change? What percentage of the salary is paid to the management team in options and/or shares? What's the previous 12-month trend for director shareholdings – have directors been buying more shares or selling their shares? If they have been selling, for what reason? Do they know something that we don't?

It's not usually that difficult to find information on director salaries, particularly for the larger companies, which is another reason that I generally favour the bigger companies. There is more transparency and greater disclosure, which means that I know what's going on at senior board level.

Of course, it doesn't always work that way and there are times where companies have managed to deceive shareholders and have not always been entirely honest. There's a great company based in California called 'Muddy Waters' which investigates publicly traded companies and exposes fraudulent activity. You should do your own research rather than following what they say blindly but it's a good early indicator and most of their stuff turns out to be true.

Thankfully and apart from a few rogues most businesses listed on the stock exchange are legitimate and because they are all subject to the same stringent disclosure requirements you should be able to smell a rat if there is a genuine cause for concern.

Assessing management is also a subjective form of assessment. I'm usually not a big fan of things which are subjective because I like order and systemisation when it comes to investing. However, this is one of the few exceptions where I think that making an assessment based on human 'feeling' is important. That's because we are looking at human behaviour and those humans at the top, whether we like it or not, are the people who will either make or break that company.

So, if I'm investing my money into a company then this effectively means that I am giving my money to somebody else to control. That's why I need to know that the person in control is worthy of my investment. I want to be assured that he or she has a good reputation, is trustworthy, has the best intentions and is committed to the business. If you can see that directors are coming and going into a business through a revolving door, that's a massive red flag.

It's a very similar risk assessment that investors perform on me before they decide on becoming a client. They want to know my track record, my previous numbers, my working history, my background and most of all they want to know why I am better placed to manage their investments than anybody else.

The same goes for the DIP.

If I don't trust the board of directors, I won't invest. And if I don't agree with the way that the business conducts itself in terms of ethics I won't invest. I want to make money for me and my clients but not at any cost. If I'm investing in a company, then I need to believe in them because I want them to win.

It's a tough balancing act because there are many businesses which I don't agree with from a moral standpoint, but they just so happen to be some of the biggest companies in the world and so it's hard to avoid them when building a share portfolio. Oil and gas companies and mining exploration companies don't exactly tick my ethical boxes. I don't think banks are exactly upstanding pillars of the community either.

Thankfully there is a surge in alternative and renewable energies and many new companies are coming into the marketplace. Hopefully, in a few years' time, they will replace the old dragons.

RISK 5 - TRADING RANGE

The fifth and final risk factor that I look at is the 'trading range'. This is the typical minimum and maximum price that the company has traded within for a given time period. In other words, it shows the recent price history of the company on a chart, giving you an idea of how the price has performed between two dates.

The time range that I find works particularly well is the past 12 months. Any longer than this entails looking at historical data, which becomes less relevant to where the business is today, and any period less than this doesn't give enough reliable data to show an obvious pattern.

A one-year window hits the sweet spot for me because it gives a very balanced picture of how the company has been trading. This is important because it tells me what the market believes to be an approximate fair value for the company during that window.

For example, if a company is trading towards the top of its trading range then this builds an invisible ceiling beyond which the price will find it difficult to penetrate. In technical terms, this is known as a *level of resistance.* Whilst a share price can move upwards and beyond this level, it does require a lot of effort. Therefore, the DIP system categorises a stock which is trading close to the top of its price range as higher risk because there is a greater possibility of a retracement.

The trading range is also important for two other reasons.

Firstly, the high and low prices (top and bottom of the trading range) allows you to calculate the dividend yield calculations at those points. In other words, it tells you the income that investors received for buying that company over the past 12 months. This is valuable information because it allows you to compare the results from your DIP analysis against the market; if your calculations are correct then you should find that it broadly corroborates.

For example, your DIP analysis may assess a company to be very low risk and so you expect to earn an income of say just 4%. However, for the past 12 months if the company has traded within a range which shows that investors received a dividend yield between 5% (top of the trading range) and 7% (bottom of the trading range), then this suggests that either the company has fundamentally changed now to what it was over the past 12 months, or that you have significantly underestimated the risk.

That's because your calculations give a 4% income calculation and yet the stock market has for the past 12 months been offering investors between 5% and 7%.

The second reason that the trading range is important is that if superimposed on the trading range of a broader benchmark index it can show you how the relative performance of the company has performed against its competitors. If the underlying stock market index has increased by say 10% in the year and the company which you are analysing has fallen by 10% in that same time frame you will see the index at the top of its trading range and the company at the bottom of its trading range. That would be a big cause for concern for me. That's because if a company can't perform well during strong market conditions the likelihood of a fall if the market takes a downturn is significantly higher.

Imagine a 100m sprinter who records a really slow time despite having the perfect weather conditions. If it begins to rain heavily and there is a huge wind pushing the sprinter back, will his performance be better or worse? It's the same with companies that perform badly when the market is going up. It means that they are more likely to perform *even worse* when the market goes down.

In fact, when it comes to comparing the benchmark index to the DIP stock that's being assessed, there is an extra useful step that I incorporated into the DIP. It's not absolutely integral to the system which is why I'm not including it in this chapter but more about that later.

As with all risk variables you need to be careful not to see the headline figure and jump to conclusions. Just because a company is trading at the bottom of its trading range definitely doesn't mean that it's a bad investment or that it's high risk. Equally, it also doesn't mean that it's a good investment and therefore low risk.

There are valid arguments on both sides to consider. A company that is in demand and doing well will be priced higher than a company that nobody wants and so a stock at the top of its trading range could be seen as a lower-risk investment. Perhaps it has fantastic prospects for accelerated growth in coming months and years which is why it's being snapped up now by savvy investors.

On the other hand, perhaps it's at the top of the range because it's become overinflated as investors have greedily scrambled because they don't want to miss the boat, in which case the price has hyperextended itself and there is actually a very high risk of it falling.

Conversely is the share at the bottom of its trading range because investors have panicked? Has this driven the price down unnecessarily in which case the risk is low and it's a good buying opportunity? Or has the price fallen because there are real problems with the company?

The real question is always about the differential between perception and reality. What's the real value and what's the perceived value? Whether a stock is at the top or bottom of its trading range is less important than the gap between what it's trading at today and what it's worth today.

However, through my research, I have found a trend which is that most companies which trade close to the top of their trading ranges, generally represent a greater level of risk to the investor and should be avoided. Therefore, I assign a high risk to stocks at the top of their trading range.

This fits in with the core of the DIP strategy which is all about price movement within two price points. That's why, with all other things being equal, you should always favour buying at the bottom of the range and selling at the top of the range. Even on those few occasions where a very high company price might be justified, there's usually a good chance that amateur investors have still driven up the price artificially beyond its true market value. For each one time that I see a price pushing through its resistance level (known as a 'breakout'), I also see at least half a dozen stocks failing to break through their resistance levels and then quickly declining.

Trading ranges are one of my favourite ways to invest, particularly in sideways moving markets, and have in fact been my staple strategy for many years. Therefore, to be able to incorporate it into the DIP strategy has given me a great deal of pleasure.

RISK RATING

Now that we have conducted a full risk assessment, we can assign a number for each of the five risk variables. There are a number of ways that you can do this depending on how intricate you want the scoring system to be.

I decided that each spoke of the wheel would be awarded between 1 and 3 points according to how risky it is. For example, if a company has a very high dividend cover it will earn 3 points but if it has very little dividend cover then it will earn only 1 point. The same applies to the other four spokes. Depending on how detailed you want to be you can operate a 1 to 5 or even 1 to 10 scoring system. I have found that 1 to 3 works best for what I was trying to achieve from the DIP which was simplicity, ease of use and efficiency.

If I was to use this strategy to manage large numbers of positions and for potentially hundreds of investment accounts, I had to ensure that it wasn't overly complicated. Besides, I also knew that complicated strategies rarely worked and so complicating things without the evidence that it could definitely improve performance, was not a good idea. In the past I had always thought that the more complex that I could make it, the better it would be, that's a mistake that many traders make in the first years of their careers. After the first decade, common sense begins to kick in.

I also liked the 1 to 3 because it denotes a traffic light system. 1 means red or 'stop', 2 means amber or 'get ready' and 3 means green or 'go'. Once again, simplifying complex financial matters helped me considerably over the years to make better investment decisions.

The great thing is that I also managed to build a system in a way which allows you to reflect *your* own appetite for risk. That's because you can be as soft or stringent as you like with the variables.

The advantage of flexibility really can't be overstated.

The markets sometimes throw out beautifully designed patterns for investors to follow, which are repeatable and predictable. But sometimes they throw out a lot of noise and pictures which are completely random and have no logic or reason. That's why flexibility is so important.

You should adapt your trading style according to the market conditions for that period of time. Sometimes you will need to be more stringent in your criteria whilst other times you can afford to be less stringent because the opportunity might be too good to pass.

If you follow a 'strict' approach, then fewer companies will pass the test and so you will not trade as often. This means less trading costs and less time spent in managing those positions. It also means that the probability of success is likely to be greater. Therefore, if you have a low propensity towards risk and don't mind trading very infrequently then that's the best way for you *personally* to implement the DIP.

The downside is that you will probably be leaving a lot of good investment opportunities on the table which can be frustrating. So, even if you are a very low-risk investor be flexible when you need to be.

Remember that when the system is working well and you're getting good results, the market conditions are favourable, and that can only happen for a period of time. That's why you should double down and really try to capitalise on those opportunities in that window of time.

If you only ever want to invest in companies which satisfy the most stringent of risk criteria, it's like waiting for the perfect goal-scoring opportunity when the football is sitting in front of an open goal and the goalkeeper is nowhere to be seen. It doesn't happen very often but when it does it's hard to miss. That's great but that scenario might only happen once or twice a year which isn't enough if you want to generate consistent profits from your portfolio.

Consider what is the right balance to give you the best of both worlds, to satisfy your risk appetite whilst understanding the importance of taking opportunities even if they are not all guaranteed goals. This means that you need to get comfortable to sometimes shoot from outside of the penalty box.

Also, you don't need to rush in. Play around with the numbers so that you can get an idea of what low, medium and high risk might look like for you. The way to do this is through understanding the risks and then assigning a *weighting* to each of the five risks according to your requirements.

RISK WEIGHTINGS

Not to be confused with risk 'ratings', the risk *weighting* refers to what level of importance i.e. 'weight' you place on each of the risk variables. For example, you might place more weight on let's say, the strength of the management team than perhaps you do on where the price sits in its trading range or maybe the market capitalisation is the most important factor to you when assessing risk.

As you already know I regard the dividend cover as the number one risk variable. This means that if I see a green traffic light for dividend cover, I might be prepared to overlook the fact that the share price is trading at the top of its trading range or that the CEO has changed twice in the past 12 months.

With my own clients, I also like to balance things up so if I am going to invest in a red zone for risk variable 2 (i.e. a smaller company that's trading on the AIM Market) then I am likely to do so only if that same company is in the green zone for at least two of the other variables, i.e. let's say that it has a very strong dividend cover (variable 1) and it has very good cash flow (variable 3). In this way, it balances things up.

Obviously, I manage not one but hundreds of client portfolios. Not all of them use the DIP because not everybody is looking for income. However, for those who do use the DIP, the way that I implement it depends on the individual's risk profile and investment objectives. This means that how I implement the DIP strategy could be very different to how you might implement it. Obviously, I need to be even more flexible in my approach to ensure that the variation of the DIP is suitable and appropriate for my investors. For example, some of my clients like the AIM market whilst others will only consider the lower risk FTSE100 companies. And even within the FTSE100, there are some clients who may only want to invest in one or two specific sectors or wish to avoid sectors altogether such as mining for example.

You don't have to worry about any of this because you are only investing for you.

So, don't worry if you measure risk in one way and somebody else measures it in another way. Two investors can measure risk in different ways, and they can both be right. One is no better than the other.

The important thing to master is what I call 'consistent flexibility'. It sounds like an oxymoron because the two terms appear to contradict each other. However, you can be consistent and flexible at the same time – be consistent with *how* you measure risk but be flexible and shift all of your calculations when you need to adapt to changing market conditions.

Consistency is often tested when analysis moves from the objective to the subjective. The danger is that if you see a company that you really like, you may find yourself becoming less strict on the risk variables. In other words, you make it easier for the company to pass the test. You need to be consistent throughout or the system doesn't work. No favouritism is allowed towards your favourite company or sector!

The only time that you should change the risk variables including how they are measured and weighted is if either your personal circumstances have genuinely changed, or the overall market risk has changed. Otherwise, stick with your game plan. The way to do this is to define the parameters for each risk variable at the beginning i.e. what is your definition of the red, yellow and green light zones for each of the risk variables? This will stop you from cheating later.

Once your strategy is defined, have confidence and stick to it. Your system should work if you follow the process correctly and if it doesn't work then it will tell you very quickly, usually within the first few trades. However, if it works to begin with and then doesn't do quite so well after a while, don't think it's the system at fault. It's almost certainly that the market dynamics have changed which will happen from time to time. You just have to be patient and wait for things to settle down again before you begin trading.

One of the worst things that you can do is to constantly change your system to follow the market. That never works. If you are not sure, then just step back and paper trade for a while with some Monopoly money until you are confident that the system is back to its winning ways.

MEAN RISK RATING (MRR)

To give the Mean Risk Rating (MRR) some meaning let's apply it to a real business. Let me tell you a quick story.

When I was just a kid, about 7 or 8 years old, my father bought a tiny, greengrocer's shop in a run-down area of Coventry. It wasn't very much at all, just a small, family business that sold fruit and vegetables, but it meant the world to me and my family. My Dad wasn't well at the time and we didn't have a lot of money. In fact, I remember that we didn't even have enough money to change the painted sign on the front of the shop which read 'DAVID'S'. Sadly, my father passed away a few years later when I was just 11. Shortly afterwards the business failed, and bailiffs were soon knocking at the door. My poor Mum had many sleepless nights and it wasn't long before the shop was closed down. We sold it for £1. That's right: one pound.

Nearly forty years later, and I finally have an opportunity to bring that little magical shop back to life. However this time it's no longer a little greengrocer's in a crime-infested area but instead, it's become a thriving, multi-billion pound, FTSE100 company which pays a dividend. It's amazing what an imagination can do!

So, let's take the example of David's Plc for our risk rating and assume that it has achieved the following scores on the risk variables.

From the table, you can see that it has a medium dividend cover, a low market capitalisation, very good cash flow, a very strong management team and it's currently priced in the middle of its trading range.

RISK VARIABLE	HIGH RISK	MEDIUM RISK	LOW RISK
DIVIDEND COVER		2	
MARKET CAPITALISATION	1		
FREE CASH FLOW			3
MANAGEMENT			3
TRADING RANGE		2	

The next step is to calculate the *mean* risk rating by simply adding up the numbers and dividing by 5.

This will give a MRR of 2+1+3+3+2 = 11/5 = 2.2

This is simply the average risk across each of the 5 variables. Now you have a specific value which demonstrates *your personal assessment* regarding the risk of the company. The higher the number, the lower the level of risk.

This number is fed into spoke 2 of the DIP Wheel.

CHAPTER 8

SPOKE 2 - COMPENSATION YIELD

BUY COMPENSATION YIELD (BCY)

The Buy Compensation Yield (BCY) Table is one of the most important tools in your trading itinerary. That's because it takes the MRR values and assigns a proportionate compensation dividend yield. I'm not including my own personal BCY Table in this book because I believe that it's important that you build your own. However it's also not the sort of information that should be taken lightly because armed with this data, you may well be tempted to start implementing the DIP before you're ready.

It's dangerous to have the exact numbers that I use without really knowing how to use them properly and testing them fully before you commit. After all there's real money involved at this stage because if you're going to use the table, it means that you're investing; so suddenly the risk now becomes very real. Up until this point we have only been talking about theory, but with the BCY table we quickly move into potentially either making a lot of money or losing a lot of money. It's like being handed the keys to a Ferrari before you pass your driving test. That's a scary proposition and should only be considered after enough time has been spent on paper trading and stress testing. Otherwise it becomes more like gambling than investing, even if you are following a tried and tested strategy.

It's also important that you don't just follow my table but create your own.

That's because your BCY table numbers should be different to mine depending on how and when you implement the DIP. If you choose to trade in particularly volatile (elastic) stocks like dividend-paying AIM companies then the range will be far greater than the more inelastic stocks such as passive, FTSE100 utility companies. The table will need to reflect this differential.

Similarly, if you trade during heightened volatile market conditions where fear is greater than usual, this also needs to be reflected in the numbers on the BCY table.

Your table therefore should have reasonable scope for movement whenever it's needed. Remember that nothing is perfect in trading, so your goal is for consistency.

If you really want to know my BCY table and the exact numbers that I use, I do make it available to my students. However, I'm sure you can understand why that's a very different proposition. Individuals who are going to spend the time and effort to educate themselves fully on an investment strategy which includes learning all of the concepts in full, are always going to be better prepared when it comes to handling specific system details like the BCY data. They have enough of the background knowledge and training to make the data work for them.

And in any case, my students are still encouraged to build their own table even if they have my numbers to follow as a template. It's a fun and fantastic learning curve that any investor should go through. I know that we all want to make money, and there's nothing wrong with that, but the journey should be as much fun as the destination.

This particular journey also happens to teach us one of the most important rules in investing which is to understand the beautiful relationship between risk and compensation yield.

Let's take David's Grocers Plc as an example. If it had an MRR of say 2.2, your BCY data might assign a dividend yield of say 5.8%. This means that if the dividend yield is below 5.8%, the compensation that an investor receives would be insufficient for the risk that he has to assume in buying that stock.

Obviously the higher risk stocks require greater compensation than the lower risk stocks. Therefore if David's had an MRR of say just 1.2 then this means that it's higher risk and so you need to be compensated with a higher dividend income.

Remember that a low mean risk rating means high risk, and a high mean risk rating means low risk. This may sound a little counter intuitive, but because I use the traffic light system, for me it makes more sense to think of it in this way. But you can number it in whichever way that you want. I simply numbered it this way because I tend to see higher numbers as a reason to GO forward (green) and invest and when I see low numbers, I see it as a reason to STOP (red).

You can just as easily flip the numbers around so that Red = 3 points and Green = 1 point.

Whichever way you decide to run the numbers, the important thing is to understand the relationship between risk and return.

As investors we only have those two things to think about, number one: what is the risk of the investment, and number two: how much do we need to be compensated to take on that risk. That's basically it.

Another interesting phenomenon you will find as you build your own BCY table is that the incremental differences between each level of yield (BCY) are not uniform. For example, the BCY increases gradually in certain areas but then jumps in others. When you start playing with the numbers you will find the same thing happens to yours. This is because the majority of trades sit within a certain medium risk zone, typically between say 5% and 6%.

This means that the companies which fall either in the low-risk or high-risk zones i.e. pay less than 5% or more than 6% are in the minority and therefore are treated differently.

If a company falls into a high-risk zone, the DIP system demands disproportionately more compensation (a higher BCY) from that company – effectively the company is being penalised for falling into the high-risk zone. Similarly, a company will be disproportionately rewarded for being in the low-risk zone – the system doesn't require anywhere near as much compensation so the BCY jumps lower.

The relationship between risk and **compensation** yield is therefore not constant. That's powerful because up until this point I had always considered risk and return as something that broadly moved in equal increments albeit inversely.

The BCY table is also powerful because as investors we all make both a conscious and subconscious judgement when we evaluate risk. However, very rarely do we quantify it as a single number and even more rarely, do we ever write it down on paper.

That's why I found this exercise so empowering for my investment strategy. As an investor if you don't quantify the risk with real numbers it means that the risk has less significance, it's not real, and it changes very quickly with the investor's mood. You always need to document these important numbers so it's in black and white. Once you assign a number to the risk and write it down you are less likely to change it – suddenly an abstract thought in your head becomes real.

But remember that neither risk nor return have any level of importance on their own, and it's only when you bring them together that you can make sense of either of them. It's only the relative positioning of each one to the other that we should care about.

Risk without return is like the yin without the yang. It doesn't work.

The relationship between the mean risk rating and level of compensation is what is important.

If the BUY COMPENSATION YIELD is the (income) reward required to take on the risk of buying this company, then we also need to see the other half of the picture, the SELL COMPENSATION YIELD.

SELL COMPENSATION YIELD (SCY)

The Sell Compensation Yield (SCY) is the dividend yield of a stock when it no longer becomes attractive. It's the opposite of the BCY.

In other words, in the same way that there is a dividend yield which is the minimum % that *you* need to receive in order to be compensated for the risk, there is also a minimum dividend yield which *other investors* need to receive in order to be compensated for the risk.

The BCY is your number and the SCY is the number for every other investor.

For example, if I believe that I need at least 6% in order to be compensated for buying David's Grocers Plc, then I need to also consider what the dividend yield (%) might need to fall to before it no longer becomes attractive to new investors.

If the company's dividend yield falls from 6% to 5%, that is obviously going to discourage some income-seeking investors to buy. All things being equal you would expect that a fewer number of investors will be attracted to a 5% yield when they can buy a similar company which pays a 6% yield.

Now, what happens if the yield falls even further to 4% or even 3%?

Yes, of course, then you would expect even fewer buyers as more investors look elsewhere to put their cash.

So you see, as the dividend yield continues to fall, the level of investor appetite also falls. Fewer and fewer investors will see David's Grocers Plc as a good buying opportunity until at some point there will be more sellers than buyers. This takes us back to the tipping point which I explained earlier.

The question, therefore, is what is the *minimum* dividend yield that most investors expect to receive. This is effectively the Buy Compensation Yield for new investors. Therefore your Sell Compensation Yield is the Buy Compensation Yield for other investors.

The next question is how do we find the SCY?

From my research, I have found that there are a couple of different ways in which we can do this.

One way is to work through the Risk table again. This is unnecessarily complex and time-consuming because it involves shifting the propensity of risk downwards for all the variables. I do still sometimes use this approach and it does work well but it is labour intensive. Therefore, and after a lot of testing, I looked at the common numbers that kept coming up over and over again and realised that there was a clear pattern. The solution that I found was remarkably simple and offered a much easier solution which works just as well and takes no time at all.

I simply deduct 15% from the BCY. Like all trading strategies you need to find what you might think of as the 'sweet spot' where the highest % of trades run through – it's where the bell of the distribution curve is at its highest.

$$SCY = BCY - 15\%$$

It's as simple as that.

If the dividend yield falls by 15% from the BCY, this means that the dividend yield for many, <u>new</u> potential investors would be too low to entice them to buy. Of course, there will always be buyers at any price and so we are not looking to capture the last buyer – we are trying to find the point where the majority of investors would say no to investing. That's what we are interested in knowing.

Also, the good news is that this % approach is adaptable to suit an individual's risk profile.

For my risk-averse clients, I can <u>reduce</u> the 15% to say 10%. In other words, if the dividend yield dropped by only 10% from the original BCY that I originally secured, then this would be the SCY.

This means that my client will be holding the stock for a shorter period which will reduce their risk (it also reduces their potential capital profit).

Conversely, if I have a client who has a higher appetite for risk, I might have a SCY which is 20% less than the BCY. This means that my client will hold the company for longer which increases their risk but also increases their potential capital profit. More about how this works later in Spoke 3.

DON'T WORRY ABOUT YOUR DIVIDEND YIELD – WORRY ABOUT SOMEBODY ELSE'S YIELD

Remember that the SCY is for <u>new</u> investors only, which is all that you should care about. As odd as this sounds, the DIP shows that the best way to predict price action is to completely forget about what dividend *you* are receiving and think only about what dividend yield *other investors* will earn.

A lot of people make the mistake of only caring about the dividend yield that they receive. Therefore, if an investor buys a share with a yield of 7% and the share price increases in value which pushes the dividend yield down to say 4%, the investor will typically not care about this fall in yield because he or she is still receiving 7%. In fact, when I speak to my own clients, they often say that they feel quite proud of themselves for picking the stock when it was cheap and have guaranteed themselves a regular income of 7% when other investors will now only receive 4%.

In fact, investors become even MORE attached to a high-income yielding company because they know that other investors can't get the same deal that they have so they don't want to let go. They become over-protective of their investment and because they have seen their capital value also appreciate the whole trade takes a life of its own and becomes a permanent fixture in the portfolio.

But yet, the optimal investment strategy is to become LESS attached to the company. That's right – the more money you make in terms of capital the less attached you should be. The greater the differential between the income that you receive and that which new investors receive, the less attached you should be. You should be MORE willing to sell your position, not less willing.

The problem is that most amateur investors don't think of it this way. They don't care about the (measly) 4% that other investors will get if they buy the company because they believe that the 4% is not affecting them. This is a mistake because 4% *does* affect them indirectly.

You see a low yield has a **serious** impact on the level of buying interest that other investors will have in the company which you already hold. If the yield keeps falling, then fewer and fewer investors will want to buy that company. Also, as the price continues to increase this will lead to more potential sellers who are inclined to make a profit. A dangerous combination of fewer buyers and more sellers can only lead to one result – a fall in the share price.

That's why the DIP works so well – it forces you to ignore your own yield and think about the new investor's yield, something which most people never do. By looking at what other investors might be doing, you can gauge investor sentiment which in turn will help you to predict buying and selling patterns, which leads directly to price action.

Whatever preconceptions you might have had before about investing, put them in the bin and reprogramme your brain to this way of thinking. This one psychological switch (thinking less about the return that you earn and more about the return that others can earn) will transform your investment trajectory overnight.

It's a seamless straight line that tells you everything that you need to know about when you should be buying, when you should be holding, and when you should be selling.

Now that we have the BCY and the SCY we can move onto identifying the stock's *Yield Compensation Range*.

YIELD COMPENSATION RANGE

The Yield Compensation Range shows us the range between the BCY and the SCY.

So, in the above example if the BCY is 5.5% the SCY would be $5.5 - 15\% = 4.6\%$

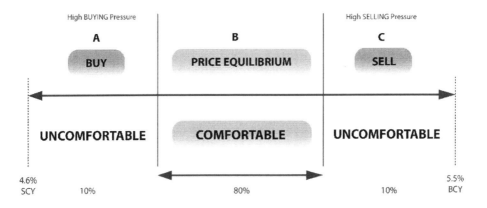

The compensation range is incredibly powerful because it shows you where the momentum is in the stock.

The stock only ever moves on **momentum** and this is *not* spread evenly in a company. The momentum is dictated by buying and selling pressure.

The maximum buying pressure takes place towards the upper end of the range i.e. as the yield reaches 5.5%.

The maximum selling pressure is at the lower end of the compensation range where the yield is at 4.6%

THE ELASTIC BAND

Think of it like an elastic band. The pressure builds and builds until it reaches a point where it snaps back. Then it goes the other way and stretches to a point before snapping back the other way.

Those two extreme endpoints are the BCY and SCY and in between, the share is at 'rest' and is most comfortable. When the share is not being extended beyond its comfort zone you will find that this is where the majority of investors participate. It's a safe place where the herds will sit. This is where retail investors congregate and make their money.

However, this is also where the smallest opportunity is to make any money. In the comfortable zone, there is no significant amount of money to be made from your investment expertise. Indeed, the only way that investors make any money if they are in this zone is because the company shares that they are holding become more profitable. But that's a different game to the one that we are playing.

The big money is at the ends of the elastic band, but as you would expect this is also where the shares will only trade for a <u>short</u> period of time. Most of the time the shares will be in the neutral zone. In fact, from my research, I found that the dividend yield will typically be in the neutral range for around 70-80% of the time. This is why the professionals trade on the edges, at the extremes of this range. They see an opportunity and they pounce on it.

This means that there is only a small window in which you can execute and take advantage of the extreme values. That's why you need to be ready and prepared and to act quickly before the price 'snaps' back to the centre.

MAKING THINGS HAPPEN OUT OF NOTHING

Most investors rely on the shares that they buy in order to make them money. They rely on strategies which are predicated on the companies which they are invested in, to make more sales, create more turnover and revenue, increase margins, and ultimately make higher and higher profits. That's how investors traditionally make money in the stock market. They buy companies which they believe will become more and more profitable in the future.

And that's fine to a point and it can make you money in the long term but it's more of a gamble because you are relying on other people to determine your success. You are betting that a company is going to continue to do well because it's done well in the past. You are hoping that a company will make more money next year and the year after. It's all a calculated bet that may or may not pay off.

The DIP strategy is different. It doesn't rely on companies to be successful. In fact, if the companies did absolutely nothing at all but just stayed static, that wouldn't affect investors who use the DIP.

What the DIP system does is far more interesting, and it's certainly a more intelligent approach.

As DIP investors we are not waiting in hope that a CEO of a company is going to make a series of good decisions so that we can profit as shareholders. We are taking control of our own financial security through understanding how investing works.

In fact, the fortune of the company will have very little impact on the performance of the DIP. The DIP simply uses the company shares as a vehicle. I would even go further to say that the DIP actually benefits if there is little change in the fortunes of a company.

That's because the DIP makes money from the price movement which is a consequence of the inefficiencies in perceived risk. It's not about making money because the company makes money. Anybody can do that; anybody can make money in a rising stock market. But making money by investing in a company which doesn't fundamentally change for a year, well that's the real secret to investing.

We already know that short term company share price moves are a result of investor sentiment and very little to do with real company fundamentals.

Therefore, the DIP simply identifies where the buying and selling activity is concentrated and takes advantage of it.

Of course, if the underlying companies also do well, then that's great for us too. We can also benefit in the same way as all of the other investors. We simply need to make the necessary adjustment on the risk parameters and shift the whole trading range upwards accordingly. If a company posts higher profits, then great, no problem; we just recalculate the mean risk rating with the new numbers.

But the point is that this is not our primary objective. We don't need to sit around hoping and praying for things that we have absolutely no control over.

We don't need to wait to be fed, we can feed ourselves from the *food cupboard* (more about that later).

MEASURE AGAINST THE CURRENT DIVIDEND YIELD

Now that you know the BCY and SCY i.e. the maximum and the minimum dividend yields, the next step is to see how these compare with the actual dividend yield.

For example, if your calculated yield compensation range runs from say 5% (SCY) to 7% (BCY) then the dividend yield of that company should currently sit somewhere within this range.

However, if it doesn't, don't worry. It simply means that the market has priced in risk differently to you. The market has decided that the company is either more or less risky than you believe it to be, and therein lies the opportunity for you to exploit.

The truth is that the market is *never* right. The price of a stock is never static, and the price moves up and down because of humans like you and me. Our buying and selling behaviours are driven by our decisions and as humans, we can make the wrong decisions. Therefore, the market price of a stock is never actually the right price for the stock – either it's too expensive or too cheap.

This means that there is *always* an opportunity to profit. The question is how big is the opportunity and is it worth taking?

If your yield happens to be very different from the current yield this doesn't mean that you're wrong. The market maybe hasn't seen what you have seen. I know this sounds hard to believe but yes, it's true – you can be right, and the market can be wrong.

That said, if out of 10 companies that you analyse, none of their dividend yields are within the compensation ranges that you have calculated, then, of course, that should worry you and it probably means that *you* are wrong. It means that you are either being overly harsh or soft in your risk assessment, in which case you should make the necessary adjustments in your risk variables.

When you set up the DIP strategy for the first time you should play around with the numbers.

You will soon get a feel for what is 'fair value' and you can then build the DIP around those values. You will then soon realise if you are being unduly harsh or soft in your assessment. It's a useful starting point just to have a basic template to work from.

Remember that the stock market will price in risk according to *all* of the factors in the marketplace at that time, not just company-specific variables.

Once you have a feel for how you should be assigning the risk variables, you will find that the dividend yield of any company will sit within your Yield Compensation Range. It may be at the top or bottom end of that range but in most cases, it should sit within it.

Now you are ready to move onto the magic, Spoke 3, my favourite step in the DIP System.

CHAPTER 9

SPOKE 3 - REVERSE-ENGINEERING THE PRICE

So now we get to the fun part because this is where we finally get to make some money from all of our hard work.

The first two spokes of the wheel can be a little daunting, especially if you are new to investing. You might also find it a little overly technical if you are not an experienced trader, but don't be concerned by that. It's like anything, habitual practice becomes the norm eventually and you will look back realising how easy it actually was, even if it may not feel like that right now.

And if it's not been very technical for you, then you can sit back and relax – because the rest will hopefully be a piece of cake.

Spoke 3 is all about reverse engineering. It's about taking the BCY and SCY numbers and then working backwards to find the answer to that all-important question, when to buy and when to sell.

But first, we need to find some important pieces of information.

DIVIDEND PER SHARE

Until a company announces a dividend it's impossible to say for sure what the dividend will be.

Companies typically announce what their upcoming (next) dividend is but do not disclose the dividend after that first one. For example, a company might disclose an interim (half-yearly) dividend but not announce the full dividend. This initially created a bit of a problem for me and my system because the DIP strategy is obviously based on the dividend and without that information the system can't run those all-important calculations.

But then I realised that it didn't matter because all investors are in the same boat and they make their investment decisions based on the information that is available. Therefore, if you only know the next dividend then you are not being disadvantaged because that's the same information that other investors are making their decision on.

Instead, the DIP System was able to circumvent this problem by the simple assumption that the second dividend payment would be equivalent to the like-for-like dividend payment the previous year. Therefore, if last year a company paid a final dividend of 10p per share and an interim dividend of 5p per share, then it would be sensible to assume that if it paid an interim dividend of 5 per share this year, that it would pay a 10p final dividend per share.

In the absence of any company news to suggest otherwise, this would make perfect sense.

Similarly, if the company paid a 6p interim dividend per share, then it could be expected that the final dividend would be 12p per share (maintaining the relationship that the final dividend is twice the interim dividend).

In some cases, the company will announce the two future dividend payments ahead of time which is also fine because then you don't need to make any estimations. But don't be afraid of estimating a forecast dividend — after all, it's what everybody else around you is doing too.

The dividend that has already been announced can be added to the historic dividend that was paid in the previous year to give an estimated total dividend to be paid out for the year ahead.

The DIP, therefore, uses a forward (future) and part trailing (historic) yield.

Of course, if the company has made news announcements hinting that it might increase (or decrease) its dividend from last year, then this needs to be taken into consideration when calculating. You can either increase or decrease the dividend yield accordingly.

The good news is that companies typically don't like to shock the market with unexpected news, especially bad news and so usually you can make a reasonable estimation on what the total dividend will be for the year ahead.

If there is a lot of uncertainty regarding a dividend or a company regularly changes the dividend amount then I would probably suggest avoiding that company altogether. That's because your calculations are likely to be more accurate if the data is fairly static. Remember that you are not trying to make money from corporate news, you are trying to make money in the *absence* of any news.

Besides, there are plenty of companies where the future dividend pay-outs are quite predictable and so it's important to only buy those companies where you have a pretty good idea of what the dividend per share will be.

Once you have the dividend per share information and your Buy and Sell Compensation Yields, you now have everything that you need to calculate the price.

PRICE

Now, this is where it gets even more exciting (yes, I am an excitable person even at the quietest of times).

Finally, we can answer that eternal question that has been sought after by investors since the beginning of time - *when to buy and when to sell.* Wow, that's powerful.

With absolute clarity and precision, based on your calculations, you can know <u>exactly when to buy and when to sell stocks from </u>any company that you have chosen to invest in.

We do this using the following simple equation:

We already know that the dividend yield is calculated as follows:

$$\text{Dividend Yield (\%)} = \frac{\text{Dividend Per Share}}{\text{Price of Share}} \times 100$$

Therefore it follows that:

$$\text{Price of Share} = \frac{\text{Dividend Per Share}}{\text{Dividend Yield (\%)}} \times 100$$

And because we already know the dividend yield (remember that's the BCY and the SCY that you have already calculated) and we know the forward 12 month dividend per share we can work out the price!

Bingo! Ladies and gentlemen, we have a winner!

Finally, we have a system that tells us when to buy and when to sell.

When is the last time that you can remember knowing with a degree of reliable accuracy, the exact price to buy something or sell something? Well, with this system that's what you get.

Will it be absolutely accurate all of the time? Of course not, no system ever is.

But now for the first time, we can at least put to one side the subjective and emotional factors that always blur our judgement. Now we know when to stay in a trade and when to get out.

We don't need to second guess or worry about the price anymore. For me, this was a surreal moment.

I realised in that instant that I had found a new way to invest. It wasn't the only way, and it probably wasn't even the best way. I wasn't under any illusion that my strategy would somehow propel me into becoming the best trader on the planet, but I had been trading as a professional for most of my adult life and so I did already know a thing or two about trading. And I knew at this moment that I was onto something special.

It was a sensible way to invest, and most importantly for me, it involved a step by step process which made intuitive sense.

There was so much good about this system that it was easy for me to regard this as my best piece of work..

You'll also be glad to know that what you are reading about now in this book is even better than what I found then. That's because I have now traded this system for several years and perfected it as I have gone along. I am sure there will be further changes in the future (the best systems are always adapting) but what you have in front of you now is the most recent and best version of my creation.

Long gone were the days where I had to take out a ruler to measure the distance from point A to point B or the times that I had to dig out a protractor from my old maths school bag to measure angles on the screen.

I'm being facetious obviously, but hopefully, you see my point.

Finally, and after years of wandering through the wilderness of the stock market jungle, I had found something that I could be proud of. It felt as though it was a just reward for my time in the game. I had earned my stripes simply by the years of service.

And here I was, I had my own strategy - the DIP strategy.

However, I only really came to appreciate what I had created after I began to implement it and I could see the results for myself. The theory was great, but the real world is the one in which we all reside. The real trades, the real profits (or losses) mattered most and so that was what I dedicated myself to next.

To trade this strategy out over and over again until I could perfect it.

Worked Example

Let's look at a worked example and imagine that we have calculated a SCY at 5% and a BCY at 8%. This is typical of somebody who wishes to adopt a more aggressive risk stance as the SCY is 3% below the BCY (37.5% below the 8% BCY), which is more than the usual 15% that I base my calculations on. I am using this more extreme example for illustration purposes but in reality, you'll probably trade within a far more modest trading range.

DAVID'S GROCERS PLC

Let's assume that David's pays a dividend per share of 5p and the share price is currently 100p.

The table shows the buying and selling price.

COMPENSATION YIELD	BUYING PRICE	SELLING PRICE
SCY 5%		5p/5% = 100p
BCY 8%	5p/8% = 62.5P	

Buy Price

As we know, the Buy Compensation Yield gives the buying price because it uses the dividend yield that we need to receive to compensate us for the risk of investing in the company. In other words, it gives a level of passive income that sufficiently compensates us i.e. it allows an investor to make sense of the risk that they are going to assume in holding that stock (compared to holding cash).

So if we want to achieve a dividend yield of 8% then we need to buy David's Plc for 62.5p. Any price above 62.5p will give us a yield of less than 8%. Therefore, we now have, almost by magic, an EXACT BUYING PRICE.

Of course, if David's Plc is currently trading at say 90p then we'll have to wait a long time before the share price reaches 62.5p if of course it ever gets there at all. But more about that later.

For now, the important thing to know is that we will buy this company only if it gives us a yield of 8% and therefore this means that we will buy it only if the share price is 62.5p or less.

The price is therefore reverse-engineered from the BCY.

And this is the fundamental shift in thinking about investing. Instead of worrying about the share price, now you just need to calculate the dividend yield which will indirectly lead to you the price.

Sell Price

Now let's assume that we are lucky enough for the share price to drop to our 62.5p and we buy the shares. This means that we will now receive an 8% yield. The next step is to work out at what price to sell.

And remember that the selling price is based on the Sell Compensation Yield.

In this example, the SCY is 5% which means that the Sell Price = 100p. Your sell price can be adapted so that it is most reflected by your own personal investment strategy i.e. how aggressive (or not) you are with your requirements.

The important thing to note is that <u>you will know</u> **exactly what your sell price should be.**

AVOID THE COMMON TRAP – NEVER SELLING

When I was building the DIP, in the back of my mind was always the tens of thousands of trades that I had conducted over the years for me and my clients. When you repeatedly do something like that over and over again, across the best part of two decades, the brain builds an automatic, subconscious response to different trading scenarios. This was useful because I already knew the most common pitfalls that investors fall into. One of the biggest mistakes was never to sell. Investors had a tendency of thinking that the market would continue upwards and so they should never sell; that's the brainwashing message from the big wealth management companies.

That's why the DIP was designed to overcome this trap.

With the DIP you have a pre-determined sell price.

Having an exact exit price is important not only because it tells you exactly when to sell. It's important because it means that you are far more likely to sell. The main reason that investors don't sell is that they don't have a clear exit price in their mind. It's psychological as much as anything else. It's easy to get caught up in the whole euphoric moment of making money and forget the reason why you made the money in the first place. Just having a buy is only half of the strategy, it's only half as good as the full strategy.

As I previously mentioned, the one reason which stops investors from selling when they really should is because they focus on *their* yield and not on *today's* yield. I can't tell you the number of times that I have spoken to investors and they always the same thing "I'm getting 7% so I'm really happy".

But because the shares were bought years ago, the dividend yield *today* might only be say 4% which means that new investors would only receive 4%. In other words, there is very little incentive for new buyers to come in and buy that stock. This is usually the reason that the share price has stalled in recent years, and perhaps even fallen in value. The fact you might be getting 7% is of no relevance and artificially distorts the true 'value' of the investment. It gives you the false impression that the company is much better than it is.

As a result, the original investor ends up in this odd situation where he feels very pleased with himself because he has secured such a high, original dividend yield, but the truth is that he has very little chance of making any further capital appreciation. Yes, their shares have increased in price but because he doesn't sell, he never captures that growth. A profit is only a profit after the stock has been sold, and the cash is sitting in your bank account. Otherwise, it's just a paper profit which is no good to anybody.

The best thing to do in this situation is to go against your instinct and to sell, take the capital profit out of the position and to reinvest the larger sum of money back into another 7% yielding stock. Then repeat until you are sitting on a warm, exotic beach somewhere where you don't need to worry about investing again.

That's how to be successful in the stock market, but it rarely happens. Investors become overly attached and protective over a company for a historic yield that they secured years ago. It's like being a football manager and still playing a striker who used to score 30 goals in a season five years ago but can't hit a barn door now. You must let go of history and focus on the now. That's how the stock market works.

Nobody cares about the success from five years ago, and neither should you.

The only thing that an investor needs to think about is the HERE AND NOW and specifically there are only two questions to consider –

1. what is the dividend yield that is being paid by the company *now?* and
2. what is the likelihood of capital appreciation from *now?*

As an investor, you should demand more from your investments. There is no point in getting a 10% capital growth in your stock in years 1, 2 and 3 and then getting no capital appreciation in years 4 and 5. But that's what most investors do. They look back and say that they are still up 30% which technically they are – but they have made 0% in the past 2 years.

That's because the dividend yield at a higher price is too low to attract more investors. The explosive growth is at the start, not at the end of the elastic band.

Remember that capital appreciation only comes from one of two ways – either:

1. the company becomes more successful and increases profits or

2. there is a short-term opportunity that investors are willing to exploit (i.e. if dividend yield is at the top of its compensation range this will attract investors, thus pushing up the price).

In the absence of any changes in the underlying business, the only way to make money is through the short to medium-term price fluctuations of the price, and that is almost entirely dictated by either short-term speculators looking for capital appreciation or big investment banks and pension funds looking to earn healthy dividends for the long term.

Once again, I'm simplifying a lot of things here so as not to complicate matters unnecessarily.

But hopefully, the DIP is starting to make more sense to you on different levels, technically and intuitively, maybe even psychologically. If it's blossoming in your mind now just as a theoretical piece of work imagine how it will blossom if you use it and it makes you money.

Now, let's move on to Spoke 4.

CHAPTER 10

SPOKE 4 - PATIENCE IS A VIRTUE

I am notoriously impatient. Ask anyone who knows me, and they will most likely tell you that I'm one of the most impatient people that they know. However spoke number 4 in the DIP strategy is all about patience, and yet I'm perfectly comfortable with that. Let me explain why.

Once you have implemented the first 3 spokes of the DIP Wheel, and you have identified your buying and selling prices, there is nothing left to do but wait. In the first instance, we must wait for the share price to fall to our chosen buy price.

And yes, while that does mean that the cash that you have is not 'working' for you, that is a very small price to pay for the two significant benefits that come with waiting.

The first benefit is that after waiting patiently, we will eventually be rewarded with an investment that doesn't pay us a 4% or 5% dividend yield but one that pays us 6% or maybe even 7%.

That's a huge difference, particularly if you end up holding the position for the longer term (more than a year). The difference between 4% and 6% may *only* be 2% in absolute terms but think of it as a 50% increase in your income.

That's massive.

So, if you have a portfolio of £500,000 which generates £20,000 of annual dividend income at 4% you can now potentially have a portfolio which generates £30,000 at 6%. That's another £10,000 (50%) for just being patient. If you hold your portfolio for five years that's an extra £50,000 in income for doing nothing.

However, there is another benefit that's even more exciting, and that is of capital appreciation potential. As you know by now, the DIP Strategy isn't just about earning a high income (in fact that's of secondary importance), it's actually more about capturing the capital appreciation and that only happens if we are prepared to be patient.

Because when we wait for the price to fall, not only does the dividend yield increase but more importantly the potential for capital appreciation also significantly increases. The two go hand in hand.

Let's go back to the elastic band analogy to make sense of this.

ELASTICITY LINE

Imagine you have an elastic band that is unstretched and sitting at rest. It's at a point of equilibrium, which means that it isn't going to go anywhere.

That's how a stock looks when it is trading at 'fair value'. It's the price that the market believes fair for that company at that precise moment in time. That price should also broadly equate to a dividend yield which sits somewhere in the centre of the Yield Compensation Range. It's the most comfortable place to be for the dividend yield.

The problem is that when the stock is trading at this sort of level that's no good to you as an investor because it's not going anywhere.

So, what you want to do is to buy a stock when it's *not* at fair value and the only way to do that is to buy when the dividend yield is *uncomfortable.* That's when the elastic band is being stretched. The more it stretches and the more uncomfortable it becomes, the greater the opportunity.

To illustrate this, think of an Elasticity Line which shows the level of discomfort in comparison to the state of rest. One is at the ends and the other is in the centre i.e. at the equilibrium.

And of course, an elastic band can only be stretched so much before the pressure builds to a point where it has no choice but to return to equilibrium and to the point of rest.

Think of the movement in the elastic band as the movement in the share price.

The movement only happens when the elastic band or the share price is being pushed into a state of discomfort. In fact there are two forms of discomfort – good and bad.

GOOD AND BAD DISCOMFORT

If you buy when the elastic band has been stretched in the correct direction, from right to left i.e. to point A, the elastic band snaps back in the right direction. The price will quickly increase, and you will get fast capital appreciation until the elastic band snaps back and returns to neutral.

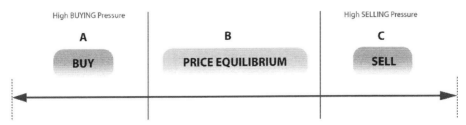

The momentum will then slow down and the price will then from this point only gradually increase. Therefore, the initial increase in price is the fastest movement to the point of equilibrium and then any subsequent increase in share price becomes slower and slower until eventually over time it should reach point C, which is your selling price.

Imagine a pendulum that oscillates from its two points of extreme. That's how share prices move.

The only reason that this pattern is not obvious is that there are external factors which upset this movement and that's why investors see charts which look completely random and unpredictable. They are only random because of random factors i.e. a company announcing a profits warning, or a Government announcing an increase in employment figures, or the European Central Bank announcing quantitative easing, or maybe a trade war between the US and China. Then of course you have the unpredictable nature of buyers and sellers who don't know what they're doing and so make poor investment decisions.

But if you cut through all of the noise and could hold everything else equal, a stock moves like a pendulum.

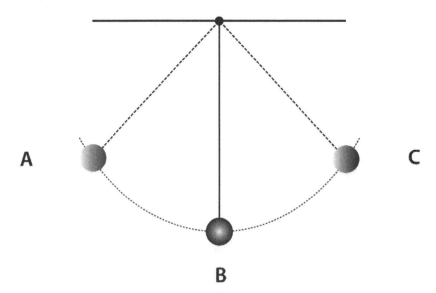

A

C

B

Therefore, if you are a buyer you need to buy at point A and sell at point C.

And the reason investors lose money is that they mix up points A and C. They buy when the pendulum has swung the wrong way i.e. when the elastic band has been stretched in the *wrong* direction. Instead of selling at point C, they buy at point C and instead of buying at point A they sell at point A. Point A is the 'bottom of the price range' and point C is the 'top of the price range' for the company.

If you have bought shares which have quickly depreciated in price almost immediately after you bought them, this is because you bought when the elastic band was stretched in the wrong direction; it's the wrong type of discomfort. Most probably you saw the price steadily increase and you didn't want to miss the opportunity. This is the classic buyer's trap which the DIP will help you to avoid.

Think of it like this; when the elastic band is uncomfortable, and therefore the price is uncomfortable, that's good for you. But it needs to be *good* discomfort, not bad discomfort. It needs to be stretched in the right direction, not the wrong direction.

Good discomfort =	Price is driven uncomfortably low and you are a buyer or
	Price is driven uncomfortably high and you are a seller
Bad discomfort =	Price is driven uncomfortably low and you are a seller or
	Price is driven uncomfortably high and you are a buyer

GOOD AND BAD PATIENCE

The problem for 90% of investors is that they are not patient on the way in (when they buy) but they are too patient on the way out (when they sell).

This goes back to the investment philosophy that I follow and teach. It's contrarian to how most of the participants trade and it's why only 10% of traders consistently make money because the other 90% keep getting it wrong.

Remember that patience is a virtue, but as with discomfort, there is good and bad patience.

Waiting for the right price is good patience. Holding a share forever just to collect the dividends without a clear exit strategy is bad patience.

You need to be patient before you buy to secure the best dividend yield and purchase price, which means that the price is more likely to snap back more quickly. This means that you won't need to be as patient because the exit price will be triggered faster.

The problem is that most investors are not patient when they buy (they typically buy when the share is trading at equilibrium or worse when it's trading at a premium to fair value) and they are *too* patient when it comes to selling because they usually never sell. Either they don't sell because they don't make enough profit (that's because of a poor entry price) or it's because they don't have a clear exit price.

The two can often go hand in hand. When investors are impatient to buy, they end up buying at a poor price, they secure a relatively small capital appreciation over a relatively long period of time, and therefore there is less incentive to sell.

The DIP works in the exact opposite way. Because it forces you to be patient on the way in, the price should quickly accelerate to the equilibrium point which gives you capital appreciation over a relatively short period of time. Therefore, when the share price reaches the selling price, the total capital appreciation is more tempting, presenting a greater incentive to sell.

Think about it; if a share offers a dividend of 5% per annum and you can make 20% in just 3 months, it would make a lot of sense to sell that share and secure 4 years' worth of dividends. However, the 20% growth is only possible as a result of being patient waiting for the share price to reach the initial buy price.

If you were impatient you might only secure a 4% dividend and therefore the capital might only go up by say 10%. Can you see how this works? It's all part of the same equation and if you upset one side of the equation, it has a direct knock-on effect on the other side.

And that's why as an impatient person, I'm actually very comfortable being patient in this case, because I know that being patient *now* means that I can afford to be less patient later.

I am prepared not to have my cash working for me now so that it can work twice as hard in the future.

So, the question is how long should you wait?

HOW LONG SHOULD YOU WAIT?

I think that a reasonable time limit is 3 months.

If you have calculated your numbers correctly and placed a realistic buy price on your chosen company, then you should really wait at least 3 months for that number to materialise. This may sound like a long time for some investors and no time at all for others, but for this strategy, it's about right.

I know some professional traders who play golf or sit on a beach for most of the year and trade only once or twice. As crazy as it sounds, they will only buy when the stock market dips by more than 10% or more from its peak and make all of their money for the year in that one hectic week of trading. It's an unorthodox approach and not one that I would use myself, but it works for them.

Therefore, waiting for 3 months is no big deal. The difficulty in waiting comes from not knowing what you are waiting for. That's when the doubt creeps in.

When you can't see what's ahead then it's easy to become impatient.

In fact, this is the biggest challenge that investors face when they try to implement the DIP for themselves. Clearly, the dividend yield using the DIP is much better than just buying a share at the current market price and so there is no question that all other things being equal, the DIP should make you more money.

So, the problem lies not in the theory behind the DIP – it's the discipline that goes behind implementing it properly.

Imagine Investor A has a £250,000 share portfolio which pays a 5% income and gives 5% capital appreciation, that's a total return of 10% or £25,000. That's very attractive in comparison to Investor B who is sitting on cash waiting for an opportunity.

And the longer that Investor B stays in cash, the more convinced Investor A will be that his investment strategy is the right one – until the stock market crashes. And then Investor A will be licking his wounds whilst Investor B will be licking his lips.

But until that happens Investor B will be enduring a lot of pain watching the market go up whilst he is earning nothing and in fact losing in real terms due to inflation. That's a mental skill in itself, how do you stop yourself from chasing the market when it's already too high?

That's why you need to wait and be patient.

Also remember that you are the person in charge of the DIP strategy, and you can change the time that you have to wait without actually changing the time. What do I mean by that?

Well, the time is affected most by the purchase price.

If you know that you are the sort of person who can't be trusted to wait, and you desperately need to see your hard-earned cash working for you then you can be less aggressive on your purchase price.

Instead of looking to buy at a price which is 30% below the market value you should move that price so it's only 10% below market value.

In other words, instead of buying when the elastic band is at full stretch, you are buying when it's only half-stretched. That has obvious pros and cons.

The main advantage is that it means that you don't need to wait, and you will be investing your money faster. You will also have more trades, which means a greater part of your portfolio is generating dividend income and capital appreciation.

That's great but it comes with a cost. The disadvantages are first that you won't capture a very high dividend yield and secondly, you won't make as much on the capital appreciation. There is a third risk which is that there's a greater risk that you will fall into a loss-making position; that's because the share price will have a greater probability to fall further.

To use the football analogy, it's the equivalent of taking more shots on goal outside of the box. A few will go straight over the crossbar and several will go wide of the post. This means that your goals scored to shots taken ratio will be less than the striker who only ever shoots from inside the penalty box although this doesn't necessarily mean that you'll score fewer goals.

However the striker who constantly takes lots of shots will disadvantage his team by allowing the opposition to regain possession of the ball whenever he misses. In the same way, when you buy too early on a trade you are going to suffer pain as you watch your stock falling in price. Now you have to wait for the price to bounce back in the same way that the striker needs to wait before regaining possession of the ball.

In terms of the elastic band or pendulum analogy, this type of premature investing means you've jumped onto only a slightly-stretched elastic band or not captured the pendulum at its highest point. Be prepared that the elastic band could keep stretching and the pendulum keeps moving *after* you have entered the trade. That's not an enjoyable journey because you are going to have to sweat it out for a while as your shares fall in value.

Of course, it's nigh on impossible for you to pick a share at the absolute lowest point. In fact, I would strongly recommend that you don't even try. It's always good to be mentally prepared for the elastic band to stretch a little after you have bought the share. That's perfectly normal. You can't expect to buy a share and then immediately for it to go up, you always need to endure some pain.

THE TOLERANCE PAIN CAP (TPC)

The question is how much pain is the right amount? In other words, what is the most amount of pain that should be tolerated, something I call the 'Tolerance Pain Cap' or TPC. Every trade should have a TPC which is the investor's signal that enough is enough and it's time to take action. Most investors have no TPC and so they make the cardinal mistake of letting their losses run instead of cutting them short. I'm not an advocate of cutting positions too early because there is always a chance of recovery but I'm a big advocate of knowing what the TPC is and **taking action** if the stock reaches it. What that action might be will depend on the trade and the circumstances which is why I don't favour a blanket sales using stop-loss orders.

The TPC depends entirely on the return to risk ratio. If I'm looking to make a 100% profit on a trade then I won't mind if the share price drops by even 25%, because I'm potentially looking to earn a 4 to 1 return on my money. Therefore, my TPC is 25% which is going to be more prevalent with penny stocks rather than dividend-paying stocks.

With the DIP strategy and because I'm buying dividend-paying shares, I'm expecting to see a return of maybe 20% depending on the volatility of the stock. Working on a 2 to 1 basis where I am rewarded with £2 for every £1 that is being risked, this means that the downside pain that I should be willing to tolerate should be no more than between 10%. In this case, the TPC is 10%.

And, so if the price falls by more than 10%, then this would suggest that something has gone wrong and I need to take action. Stocks can fall for a number of reasons which is why at this point you need to look at what has happened. Has the stock market fallen dragging all equity prices down with it, has the company announced a profits warning, is there a big seller in the market and why is he selling, has the company hit it's ex-dividend date and so the price has dropped by the dividend? There are many different reasons but in each of those cases, there is one constant truth, which is that your purchase price was too high in the first place.

You could argue that a profits warning or a stock market crash couldn't be predicted and so it's not your fault, but unfortunately nobody cares whose fault it is. As part of the DIP calculation, we are measuring risk and need to incorporate those risks into the purchase price. It doesn't matter if those risks are not easy to predict. As investors, we have to always blame ourselves even for things over which we have no control because the market is deaf to our protests.

Once we assign blame and responsibility to ourselves, even if it feels grossly unfair, we can focus on fixing the problem. That means either waiting for the recovery or taking decisive action and cutting loose by selling and crystallising a loss.

If the price keeps falling and the elastic band keeps stretching then in a worst-case scenario, the elastic band can even snap. That's where the share price goes into free fall and the company cuts its dividend.

Remember that this is one of the major risks with the DIP strategy – that the company cuts its dividend. As long as the company maintains the dividend then it should always act as a strong support structure but if the dividend can't be relied upon then the whole strategy hangs precariously on a false assumption.

Sometimes you see companies paying a 10% dividend which looks great on paper, but they are not real. It's just a matter of time before the company announces that its next dividend is going to be slashed. This is where novice investors get caught out, they are blinded by the headline figure of 10% but don't realise that it's paying 10% for a reason. That's why very rarely will I venture into a share that pays me 10%.

Sometimes the share price does bounce back and investors can make a lot of money or on other occasions, the price doesn't move but keeps paying out a very high dividend of 10% and in some cases 15% or even more. However, it's not sustainable and it's only a matter of time before that party finishes abruptly. When you run the numbers back, you will find that the risk doesn't justify the reward. It's not about reward alone but the relationship it has with risk which is important.

The elastic band is so severely stretched that the risk of completely snapping and breaking outweighs the potential return that it might make for an investor if the band returns to equilibrium.

So, moving on, let's say that our patience does pay off and the company share price falls to reach our buying level. That's great news.

Now we get to the final spoke of the DIP Wheel, Spoke 5.

CHAPTER 11

SPOKE 5 - TIME TO SELL

If you reach this point in the DIP Wheel, (and assuming that you have not entered the market prematurely at a higher price than you should have because you were impatient), then I have some great news for you. No matter what happens going forward, you are already in a really strong position as an investor.

That's because you have secured the purchase of a low-medium risk company with a much higher than average dividend yield, which is likely to generate passive dividend income for years to come. As long as the directors of the business don't do anything stupid and the market doesn't crash then you should be able to enjoy a yield of 5, 6, 7 or even 8% from now until the 12th of Never.

However, as you know by now, that's not what we really care about. Yes, the enhanced dividend yield is lovely and not to be sniffed at. But if that's all we cared about then this strategy would be called "The Dividend Income" and not the "Dividend Income *Plus*" where the '*plus*' of course refers to '*plus capital appreciation*'.

So, yes, we are greedy, and we want more than just dividends. We want dividend income PLUS capital appreciation and that's where Spoke 5 comes into play.

And besides 'The DI' doesn't have the same ring to it as 'The DIP'.

Spoke 5 of the DIP Wheel is all about maximising the capital appreciation, and it's the biggest earner for your share portfolio. It's the step which gives me most of my happiness as an investment manager, and it's the step that gives my clients their greatest joy because it generates real tangible growth for their assets.

It's also in many ways the easiest step of all, because Spoke 5 doesn't have to happen for you to make money. That's because even if the price doesn't increase enough to reach your chosen sell price, then you are still collecting very healthy dividends.

Spoke 4 calls for patience and is difficult because you are earning nothing while you wait for a share price to fall. In contrast Spoke 5 is easy because now you are <u>being paid while you wait</u>.

And who doesn't like to be paid for sitting on their backside, watching a UFC title fight, and eating lemon cheesecake? Or is that just me?

It's the same as when you buy a buy-to-let house for investment purposes. You may not get capital appreciation straight away, but if the rental income surpasses the mortgage and maintenance costs, and you are earning positive cash flow then it really doesn't matter. You can afford to just sit tight and wait for the housing market to go up and then sell your house at a decent profit.

The only difference with the stock market is that there are no mortgage payments and there are no expenses. Therefore, the dividend income is all profit. Brilliant.

Now let's see what happens after the sell order is triggered.

AFTER THE SALE

Let's say that the price does increase and hits our sell exit point. This means that the entire DIP Wheel is completed. So, what happens now with the cash that has become available? Well, the next step is super-simple – you just repeat the whole process again.

In other words, the cash will immediately return to the share-dealing account and the money can now be used to invest in new opportunities. In fact, you should already have done your research and identified at least 10 or 20 companies with the Buy Price already calculated. In this way, the cash can immediately be ready for reinvestment and won't sit around idle.

In fact, after a while you will find that there is a pretty good chance that you could end up buying the same company, again and again, using this strategy. This is especially true in a sideways moving market where the stock market doesn't go up or down but just trades within a small trading range.

It's how a lot of chartists and technical traders make money because it relies on buying the same company at the support level, selling at the resistance level and then buying back at the support level again, and so on. The DIP works in the same way of buying, selling and then rebuying – except it has two subtle differences.

Number one, the DIP buys dividend-paying companies which means that unlike short-term traders who look for capital growth only, we get paid for waiting but they don't.

Number two, short-term traders pick the levels based on historic trading patterns whereas we use the trading pattern for guidance as only one part of the risk assessment process (risk variable 5) but our buying (support) and selling (resistance) prices are dictated by the elasticity and the extremities of the dividend yield. In both cases, our parameters are more reliable.

CHAPTER 12

FINANCIAL PHYSICS

We covered a lot of information in the last few chapters, so I just want to pause for a moment and ensure that the logic of the DIP is now really crystal clear before we move on. The best way to do that is to forget about money and finance for a moment and think about nature and the way that the world works.

In fact, such is the importance of this concept that I decided to even give it a name. I call it '*financial physics*' because it takes the principles of physics (wave theory) and applies it to the financial world.

You see, I have always seen trading as much more than just buying and selling shares. Trading closely resembles the world that we live in. It is about energy and movement. It's beautiful when you think of it like this. It literally mirrors the way that an ocean wave crashes onto a shore or how a bird flies effortlessly through the sky. There is a timing and perfection in nature that is often missed by the human eye. There is a synchronicity that we fail to see even though it's there.

The waves are not random but yet appear completely random when we watch them. In fact, all waves work in exactly the same way, with the build-up of energy passing through water and creating momentum. This momentum continues until the energy reaches a peak and where the wave reaches a crescendo, its highest point. Then it comes crashing back down and the whole process starts again.

When a bird flies through the sky it does so in periodic waves, perfect oscillations. It pushes through the air and follows a pattern, a pattern of least resistance. If you track and plot its movement on a chart, you will witness a cycle emerge. The cycle may be different to ocean waves, but the pattern is undeniable.

That's how waves work. That's how trading works. That's how all cycles work.

There are patterns and if we see and learn to recognise those patterns, we can more accurately predict what is likely to happen. That's how to make money.

The reason that ocean waves appear random is that at any given moment there are dozens of other waves of varying sizes travelling from different directions, all congregating at that exact same point in the water. There are also other factors to consider like the speed and direction of the wind, the size of fish under the sea, and the strength of the undercurrent. This is what gives rise to the unpredictability and randomness that we witness. But despite the random picture that we see, the waves themselves are perfectly predictable. It's the external influences that make the picture blurry.

In trading, we call those external influences 'noise'.

The randomness and noise from trading come from erratic human emotions – it's false data. That's because trading is a depiction of our thoughts, of our fears. Fear of losing money against the fear of missing out on a money-making opportunity. It's the collective thoughts of millions of people around the world driving buying and selling behaviours which in turn is reflected in the price.

But despite the unpredictability of human emotion and just like ocean waves the principles are very predictable. The patterns are always the same. Buy low, sell high.

We just need to cut through the noise to find the solution.

In the world of physics, a state of equilibrium is defined as a condition where there is no motion and there are equal and opposite forces in play. In other words, one force cancels out the other. That's what happens with shares and investments.

When there is an equal number of buyers and sellers in the market place the price doesn't move. It's static.

However, when there are more buyers than sellers, the price goes up. When the price goes up, the opportunity of further price increases also erodes as investors become increasingly wary of buying. Therefore, the momentum begins to slow down until we come to a standstill and, eventually, we begin to see the reversal. When a wave goes higher and higher, it is only a matter of time before it peaks and reverses.

Wave theory affects just about everything in our lives from the light that we see, to the sounds that we hear, to the vibrations that we feel. We are constantly surrounded by waves, by these peaks and dips.

And it's not just physics, but it's also in chemistry and biology.

Think about nature's way of neutralising something through osmosis. That's defined as a process by which molecules of a solvent pass through a semipermeable membrane from a less concentrated solution into a more concentrated one. In other words, mother nature has an automatic built-in mechanism which helps to neutralise things.

In the same way, there is a natural movement from hot to cold, from up to down, from fast to slow. In fact, it brings all things in motion to equilibrium. When things are at equilibrium we have a position of rest with equal and opposite forces.

In fact, almost every natural thing that you can think of in life is about equilibrium, balance and neutrality.

Things which are *extreme* are defined as such because they are unusual. By definition events which are unusual means that the event doesn't happen often and when it does happen, it happens only for a short period of time.

That's what happens to extreme dividend yields – they don't happen often, and they only remain in that state for a short period of time. The majority of the time shares like everything in this world sit in a lazy state of comfort.

I describe the DIP in this way because I want it to make inherent sense to you in the way that it does to me.

It's why I continue to use different analogies throughout this book so that the conceptual understanding of the DIP becomes so ingrained into your thoughts, that it begins to make sense on every level. My goal is for it to eventually make sense to you subconsciously, without even having to think about it.

To use another example, consider an apple falling from a tree, we know why it does that – without the support of a branch keeping the apple connected to the tree, it's pulled to the ground by gravity. And the force to bring it down is greater than the force which is trying to keep it up. This is an uncomfortable position because the forces are unequal (the downward force is greater than the upward force) and so it falls to the ground where it can experience equal forces i.e. it reaches a comfortable position of rest.

And if somebody picks the apple up and throws it into the air it will again be in a place of discomfort until it falls back to the ground again.

Shares move in the same way. In the absence of any other news, a dividend-paying share always gravitates towards a position of rest – its equilibrium or fair value. That's where the dividend yield equates perfectly to the risk being assumed by the investor. It's the Goldilocks' porridge scenario – the 'not too hot, not too cold, it's just about right'.

It's more empowering to try and forget about the DIP as being solely a financial concept and instead view it conceptually as a world of extremes against neutrality.

When we have an extreme i.e. the dividend is abnormally high or abnormally low, the natural forces will push the dividends back to a place which is less extreme and more normal. This happens through a shift in human buying behaviours, which impacts the price.

I'm not a scientist and so can't say if my knowledge of wave theory is absolutely accurate but I can tell you this. The stock market is more predictable than most people think. It leaves clues and patterns behind which are remarkably easy to follow. The difficulty is sifting through the noise.

But don't let that stop you from believing that the pattern isn't there. Hopefully, this idea of Financial Physics will resonate with you as much as it does with me.

When you see the stock market as physics, you understand that you can't control it any more than you can control the natural forces of the ocean. Therefore you realise that instead of working against it, you need to find a way to work with it. That's what the DIP has allowed me to do and will allow you to do if you let it.

You should almost be able to touch those huge, invisible forces when shares peak before they crash, it's as if cash floods in and out of the market like water floods in and out when a dam opens and closes.

If you can understand and really appreciate momentum and forces, then investing becomes so easy. You just go with the flow.

It's impossible to lose when you are on the right side of that momentum.

So, with the physics lesson over, and now that you see the whole picture let's look at the risks. Things can and will go wrong but don't let that paralyse you into fear, in fact, don't even worry about the risks. You should feel very comfortable with risk by now, and understand that risk is and always will be a part of investing as it is and always will be a part of life.

We shouldn't care that risk exists; we only need to care about learning how to manage it because things can and sometimes will go wrong.

CHAPTER 13

WHEN THINGS GO WRONG

Let's be very clear.

Quite a lot of things can go wrong with any investment strategy. Dividends can be cut, companies can go bust, the stock market can crash, wars can happen, and even a previously unheard-of virus named after a Mexican beer can put the world into lockdown. The point is sh*t happens.

But that's okay because the risk is there to be accepted and understood. In order to become comfortable with the risk you need to learn about it, and not be fearful of it. Risk should be embraced, cherished, loved. Risk is your friend, not your foe and in this chapter, I'm going to show you why.

There are several risks that the DIP strategy is exposed to and I'm going to highlight as many as I possibly can. Instead of shying away from describing the risks, I'm going to do the opposite and exaggerate them. I'm going to make the risks so outrageously dangerous that in the real world it would be unrealistic that some of these risks would happen, but I'm going to talk about them anyway.

The reason I'm doing this is to put the DIP system under a lot more pressure than it might be subject to in the real world.

I wanted to know the worst-case scenario, not just a bad case scenario. As a professional investor with a system which I believe is superior to any other system (at least that I'm aware of) in the marketplace, it would be wrong for me not to put it under immense scrutiny and pressure to make sure that it really does perform.

I have already talked about extremes and pushing boundaries when it comes to the dividend yield and price action. It would only be fair that I apply the same logic to the risks because if I can do that, and the DIP strategy still stands up, then that is very reassuring.

You can think of it as extreme 'stress-testing'. If it survives this chapter then it's ready to not only play but to compete with the big-boy strategies of the investment banks,

So, let's put the DIP system under some real pressure and see if any cracks appear.

There are five main risks that can impact the DIP Strategy.

RISK 1 – WE NEVER BUY
PURCHASE PRICE IS NOT REACHED

Let's assume that you have gone through your analysis, picked out the stocks, performed your risk assessment, worked out the dividend yield range and now you have your buying and selling prices ready to go.

You put your buy orders into the system and wait for them to get filled…and wait….and wait some more.

You might wait for 3 months and then another 3 months and maybe even 3 more months, and before you know it a whole year has passed. What's the risk to you in this scenario?

Well, it depends on how you look at it. Yes, admittedly there have been no trades, no dividends, no profits — but also, we must remember that there have been no losses – so is that a risk?

We could point to the fact that the cash could have been sitting in a bank account earning something but with interest rates barely paying anything these days this isn't really a credible argument. If we are going to say that we prefer a guaranteed 0.1% return on cash in the bank against the possibility of making 20% in the stock market, then the stock market probably isn't for us.

The biggest 'risk' is the missed opportunity but how do we quantify this?

We could be harsh on ourselves and argue that the money could have been invested in the stock market and instead of waiting for an extreme dividend yield of 7% we should have just taken the normal yield of 5% instead.

Yes, maybe that's true with the benefit of hindsight, but the whole point of the DIP is that we want a high yield, not an average yield, we want high capital appreciation, not an average capital appreciation. And in order to get 'high' of anything, it means that we have to be patient.

Now think about what would have happened if being patient was actually the right thing to do i.e. what if the stock market had fallen and by being patient we were able to miss a big chunk of that move that lost so much money for every other investor. Then of course we would have been very thankful that we had waited, right?

Having spoken to quite literally hundreds of my own clients about this topic, I recognise that the risk of not buying is very subjective and personal because it depends on the individual. For some investors, the opportunity of missing a stock market rally is far more painful than investing and risking a market downturn. For others missing a buying opportunity is not important, what's more important is not to lose anything and so they prefer not to invest during uncertain times.

This divide is only accentuated by other variables, for example, how much cash an investor holds. If an investor is 100% in cash (i.e. he holds no equities), then he is more likely to be less patient because the opportunity cost of missing out on a market rally is more significant. Compare that to an investor who only holds 10% cash (90% is already invested); this person is not going to worry as much about missing an opportunity because a rising market would mean that he can still benefit from their current exposure. Similarly, a person who relies on this portfolio to provide an income is more likely to want the money invested for dividends even if that might mean he is more exposed to a market crash, whereas somebody who doesn't rely on his portfolio is likely to adopt a more patient approach.

Both types of investors will assess risk differently.

For me personally, I like to think of risk only when I suffer a real loss that is quantifiable. If the market goes up and I miss an opportunity, then I don't view that as a risk because I haven't physically lost anything. I am no richer or poorer than I was before. If I had £100,000 sitting in the bank before that missed opportunity, then I would still have £100,000 sitting in the bank today. So, I have lost nothing in real terms.

However, if I am not patient and invest £100,000 into the stock market and the prices fall by 20% then I am now worse off by £20,000. That's money that I have really lost so for me that's a real risk.

I don't think that anybody would disagree on this point but for the sake of completeness I wanted to display both sides of the argument, albeit one of those sides is seriously flawed. We all know that real risk has to mean that you *lose* money and not investing your cash is therefore not a real risk.

In any case, now let's consider *why* the DIP strategy would not reach the buy price that you have set. Well, it can only be for one of three reasons:

1. THE INITIAL DIP PARAMETERS THAT WERE PLACED WERE TOO STRICT.

This is particularly common for both risk-averse investors and very greedy investors. The risk-averse investors place such a great emphasis on the risk variables during the risk assessment stage that they can often overestimate the risk of a company. By doing so their compensation yield calculations become unrealistically high. For example, if I am very risk-averse, I might score the risk variables so aggressively which means that I expect a dividend yield of say 8 or 9% on a company.

If that company is currently trading at a price which gives investors a yield of say 5% then the share price would have to fall by such a dramatic amount to reach the BCY that it's just never going to happen. It's just too far away. When choosing to buy prices, you have to be realistic. It would be great if we could all buy a dividend-paying 500p stock for 200p, but in reality that is almost impossible and so the buy price has to be sensible and achievable.

The greedy investors aren't necessarily risk-averse and so their calculations are sensible. The problem is that even if their calculations show a certain buy price, they typically intervene and change their purchase price, driving it down artificially. In other words, they overrule their system.

In both cases, the overtly risk-averse and greedy do themselves a great injustice. Their buy orders almost never get filled because they are expecting the elastic band to stretch to a point which is over the top and completely unrealistic.

2. WE ARE IN A BULL MARKET

The second reason that the buy orders might not be filled is that we are going through a bull market. If the stock market is rampant and continues to increase, then trying to secure shares at a discount to the market value is going to be tough. That's because everybody is buying shares, the economy is booming, stock market prices are rallying, which is driving the price up of all stocks. This is why you must be mindful of market conditions when you implement the DIP.

There is no point in being patient when the market is heading north.

Similarly, if the market is plateauing after a significant bull run then there may well be added external, downward forces to consider in which case you can afford to be more aggressive with your pricing and your patience.

For example, if the market has just crashed, and you are lucky enough to buy on a 10-year low, you need to consider the real opportunity that presents itself. Is the real opportunity here to wait for a drop in prices and then sell with a 10-15% profit? Or is it better not to wait and just buy now, even at a high price, because you know that market is going up?

A bull market means that previous trading highs are likely to be broken and so you could make maybe 30% or 40% even if the dividend yield is not so high. Which is better?

The answer is the latter and the overarching point is that you should always adapt.

Following a significant market crash, we usually witness a sharp recovery which is phase 1 of the bull market recovery. The trick is to spot this moment and then tweak the DIP parameters so that you can take advantage of the bigger price swings.

You can think of it as though the elasticity has just increased! The elastic band stretches twice as far as it did before.

You can still make money if you don't adapt, but you will make so much more if you can position your DIP strategy according to the prevailing market conditions.

That same logic applies in every other asset class – for example if the housing market has crashed where is the value as an investor? Is it in earning a rental income of 7% per annum or is it in the opportunity to make a 100% return in 3 years from capital appreciation?

3. NOT ENOUGH ATTEMPTS TO BUY

Another reason that you probably haven't made any share purchases using the DIP, is because you haven't chosen enough companies. For the DIP Strategy to work, you need to work <u>multiple</u> buy orders simultaneously. If you only try and buy one company, then you are seriously reducing the likelihood of the position being filled.

It's like when you go fishing. You will increase your chances of catching a fish if you put up multiple fishing lines. As a minimum, I would suggest that you look at 10 to 15 companies and if you are being particularly aggressive with your risk parameters and compensation yields then that number should be even higher. Remember that you are not committing to all of those positions, but you need to see which companies might get filled and which ones won't. You can always cancel the outstanding orders once you are happy that you have enough positions running.

Think of it as if you want to buy a house. The DIP allows you to be cheeky and put offers on multiple houses 20% below the market price. The chances are that most of the vendors will say no, but you might just get lucky with one of them. And that's the game that is being played here.

One word of warning - if the market does take a big, unexpected drop then you need to be prepared for the possibility that *all* of your buy orders will be filled. But don't see this as a bad thing – this is what you have been hoping for. And it means that you don't have to sit around waiting for the next few months. You could have your entire DIP portfolio built almost overnight.

This has happened to me before and actually, it's very exciting. A share market correction often triggered by a political event or another macro-economic phenomenon will help to fill a quick succession of buy orders within the space of a couple of days. In most cases, within just a few weeks the market has risen back to where it started and in the meantime, you have secured some fantastic high dividend-paying stocks and all are showing capital appreciation! That's a great position to be in.

In conclusion and regardless of the reason why we haven't managed to secure any buys, I think that we can all agree that this first risk is really not too bad. The fact is that <u>we haven't actually lost any money</u>. Yes, there is a missed opportunity to invest but still, there is no loss in your capital.

Let's move on to the next possible risk with the DIP strategy.

RISK 2 – SHARES FALL IN PRICE NO DIVIDEND CUT

Let's say that the DIP does allow us to buy the shares at our buy price. What's the risk and what happens if the share price continues to fall in value, but the company doesn't cut its dividend?

Well, think about it for a second.

If you are already an investor in the stock market who has a portfolio of shares and you're looking to buy more shares, or even if you are looking to buy shares for the first time, then you are going to expose yourself to risk the moment you purchase. This risk is directly correlated to your purchase price. If you buy shares at a price higher than their fair value, then you expose yourself to a higher level of risk.

Therefore there is no '*extra*' risk from using the DIP strategy. In fact, buying a share, fund or any other investment at a *discount* to the market value, can only be seen as a good thing because you are buying at a price lower than you would otherwise have achieved if you had just bought without waiting for the price to fall. In other words, even if a share price falls in value you are not any worse off than if you had just bought in any case. In fact, you are considerably better off.

The solution in this scenario is just to do what other buy and hold investors do, which is simply to wait and not panic.

Hence, the answer about what to do is actually very easy - just keep the stock and hold it. As you know the company will be paying you an abnormally high dividend in comparison to what it usually pays out, and because you have captured this high yield, you're in a much better position than all of the other investors who bought the same company share at a higher price than you.

This is the one and only time that you will hear me agree with the 'buy and hold' investment fraternity and it's the one time where the DIP System marries up very closely with what most investors are already doing. The only difference is that investors using the DIP will be receiving maybe 20% or 30% more annual income than other investors from the higher dividend yield that has been captured. Whilst most investors are being paid let's say an average of 4% in dividend income, the DIP Investors are probably getting paid 6% or more to hold the same company with the same level of risk.

And so if the share price falls in value, then you should be very comfortable to hold. The DIP temporarily becomes a 'buy and hold' strategy except it's infinitely better than the normal buy and hold approach.

As long as you are confident that the company is unlikely to cut its dividend, then your job is to steel your nerves and collect your dividends. Simple.

That said, if the price does stay below your purchase price and continues to drift lower then there is a reliable risk mitigation strategy which you can implement. This is much better than not following the DIP strategy because most investors who have lost money on their shares don't have a clear exit strategy, they just hold and hope.

The risk mitigation strategy that I have developed and incorporate within the DIP is something that I call 'Recalibration'.

RECALIBRATION

If you find that you are sitting in 'negative equity' on one of your DIP purchases i.e. the current price is below your purchase price, and even if there is no imminent danger of the dividend being cut, you still need to consider why the share price is trading so low. This is especially true if the price hits your TPC because at this point action has to be taken.

The reason for the price fall is usually because we simply miscalculated the risk of the company and therefore our purchase price was too high. In other words, you bought prematurely and at a time when the elastic band wasn't fully stretched. You should have waited for the price to fall further.

And if that's the case then it would follow that your sell exit price must also be wrong. That's because there is only so much stretch in the elastic band, and there is only so much swing in the pendulum.

So now it's important that you *adjust* your sale price.

The mistake that many investors make is that they always aim to make the same return on their capital but what they don't realise is that their return is based not on the entry price but the *lowest* price that their shares fall to (during that particular trading window).

For example, if I buy a stock for 400p and have a target price of 480p (20%) that's quite sensible but if the stock falls to 360p then suddenly the stock needs to rally from its low point of 360p to 480p which is 120p or 33%, clearly a less realistic target.

So, remember - if the entry price is too high, and the shares fall in value then you need to accept that the sale price is not going to be what you had hoped it would be.

I can't tell you how many portfolios that I have seen over the years where investors are losing 50% on shares that they bought years ago and still they refuse to sell until the price goes above their purchase price. A lot of those companies don't even pay dividends!

That's why when you get a trade wrong the first thing that you should do is to simply put your hands up and accept your mistake; then you need to find the quickest way to exit the trade with minimal loss.

Don't worry about making a profit, that ship has already sailed. Now the name of the game is to try and recover your capital as quickly as possible and get the hell out of there – there are plenty of better opportunities that deserve your attention.

And when your entry is really bad, let's say it's on the wrong side of the elastic band then the same rule applies, except now it becomes a disaster recovery scenario. This means that the opportunity for recalibration is gone and you will need to suffer a loss on the trade. That's okay, if you messed up your calculations and entry price then you need to pay a penalty for it, the trick is to keep the penalty to a minimum and don't let your ego get in the way of thinking that you can find a way out and make a profit. You can't.

The ability to manoeuvre along the elasticity line and adapt the exit sell price according to how accurately you have entered the trade is a process that I refer to as 'recalibration'. You are recalibrating the calculations in the way that a shooter might recalibrate his gun if the first shot was wildly off target.

Making a bad judgement call on the entry price is likely to happen from time to time. So, it's better to expect that now and be prepared for it.

It's not unusual for private investors to find it difficult to accept losses. In fact, most private investors would rather hold a company forever rather than to suffer a loss. That's crazy. It's the equivalent of saying that you can never accept that you were wrong.

Sometimes that's because of denial and sometimes it's because of ego, in the worst cases it can be both. Investing in the stock market is a great equaliser amongst humans. It can humble the biggest of egos in a second. We all want to be right but it's just not possible, so my advice is always aim to be less wrong.

Recalibration of Elasticity Line

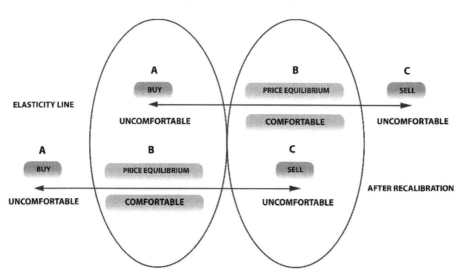

The top line is your initial calculation. When the stock is trading at point B, you do your DIP calculation and decide that you want to buy at point A. A few weeks later the stock reaches point A but instead of travelling to the right in the direction of A-B-C where C is your sell point, it goes the other way.

The price goes left along the elasticity line i.e. it continues to fall in price.

Because your initial return to risk calculations for the DIP should be broadly accurate there is no need to change the relationship between the entry and exit price. There will be some difference to the calculation because if the price differential (sell price – entry price) is based on lower prices, then this will mean a higher % change. That can be corrected if the differential is large enough but that's beyond the scope of this book.

The most important thing is to simply shift the entire elasticity line to the left.

By recalibrating, the new sell price shifts to the left where the original equilibrium price was. In other words, the original point B now becomes my new point C.

Thankfully the trade still gives me a profit, but obviously not as much as I had intended. When a share price is falling our focus needs to move from making a profit to *reducing* the risk. That's how professionals beat the average investor. Damage limitation and focussing on reducing losses is one of the quickest and easiest ways to improve profits.

The degree of recalibration is also up to you.

If the share price looks as though it is really struggling, then you have the option to shift the entire elasticity line even further to the left so that the original buy price (point A) now becomes your new sell price (point C). This means that you won't make or lose anything on the trade, but you will get back your original investment (less any dealing costs).

In the past, I have done this for my clients and once again it's nothing to be ashamed of. It either means that I completely misjudged the risk or that the stock market has fallen and there was a drop across the board on all equities.

Remember, that whatever happens and if there is no risk to the dividends being cut, then you remain in a strong position because you continue to collect the income. There is no reason to panic sell. However if I can get back my original investment and perhaps collect one or two dividends along the way whilst waiting, knowing full well that it was essentially a bad trade in terms of my risk calculation, well I would be happy with that result.

It's all about risk management. The great thing with the DIP is that as long as you can wait it out until the share price recovers, there is very little downside. Over time you can of course accumulate enough income through dividends to post an overall profit but this can take years and so the missed opportunity cost is too great.

However, for me and my clients, that's really not enough. If capital is tied up in stocks which are not doing anything other than producing an income, then I would rather get out even if that means taking a small loss or at 'break-even', sometimes known as 'washing its face'. If you are thinking about using the DIP you have the option just to sit it out and wait, which is also perfectly acceptable, but you still need to be mindful of dropping your exit price to a more realistic level.

All of the above is only possible through a recalibration of the exit price.

RISK 3 – SHARES GO UP
WE SELL TOO EARLY

Now that we have considered what happens if the shares go down in value, let's consider what happens if the shares go up in value. Specifically, what's the risk if the price reaches our sell price, executes our order but then continues to increase?

Let's say we have bought David's Plc at a great price with a great dividend yield. We hold the position for a few months and collect one semi-annual dividend payment of 3% (6% for the year). The share price goes up during this time and reaches our sell price target which happens to be 18% above our buy price level.

So, we now have a situation where within the space of 5 short months we have made a total return of 21% less any charges.

Now I will ask this question. If we are considering the risks involved in the DIP strategy and it's just made us a 21% profit in 5 months, then where is the risk?

We come full circle back to Risk 1 where there was a missed opportunity. There's no financial loss and we are not losing any money. It's just that we could have made more money.

That's why it would be harsh to regard this as a 'risk' even though I'm including it in this section just to stress-test the theory beyond what is deemed fair and reasonable.

If we sold David's Plc and made 21% profit and it continues to increase, say by another 10%, of course, that would be frustrating. But 'frustration' isn't a risk. We might even make the mistake of assuming that had it not been for the DIP strategy we could have made another 10% profit.

But that's not true.

Firstly, we must remember that it was the DIP that gave us the low purchase entry point in the first place. Without the DIP the likelihood is that we would have purchased the stock at a much higher price, therefore the return wouldn't have been anywhere near 18%, perhaps closer to 8%.

Secondly, we need to consider that the DIP forces the sale.

This is important because if we hadn't used the DIP strategy then we probably wouldn't have sold at the higher price which means that we wouldn't have captured the profit. It's been seen time and time again that most investors don't know when to sell and rarely sell at the top of the market. The DIP, therefore, plays an important role in pushing us to sell.

It's a romantic notion to think that we would just sell of our own accord, and at the top of the market but as we know that very rarely happens. And if we don't sell, then there is a good chance that the shares could fall in value again in which case that extra 10% counted for nothing because we didn't capture the profit anyway.

Thirdly, and perhaps the most important thing to remember is that a profit is a profit is a profit.

That's right, I did just say that three times. In fact, with your consent I will throw one more in just for good measure - it's a profit. Nobody ever got poor taking a profit and that's what we must remember as investors. I used to kick myself when I felt that I had sold a stock 'too early', but not anymore.

If you are following a system that generates consistent profits, then you shouldn't be greedy. The DIP already is set up so that it allows you to be greedy by buying at below market value and so we mustn't be greedy on top of greedy, that's just plain wrong. For every time that I thought that I had sold too early, there are at least half a dozen times where I am glad that I sold when I did.

I used to feel bad about not making as much money as I could have from a trade but then I realised that the stock market is there for everybody. It makes me feel a little bit better in an odd sort of way. If I can make 20% and another person who needs the money more than me can make 10% then isn't that better than if I make 30%?

I know that it doesn't quite work like this, but it makes me feel better and puts me in the right mindset so I encourage you to do the same. To summarise, if a risk is defined as *losing* money and we don't lose money but make money, clearly there is no risk.

This DIP is shaping up well, so now let's turn up the heat and put it under some real pressure.

RISK 4 – MARKET CRASH

Risk 4 is the Armageddon situation that every investor is fearful of. It typically occurs once every 10 years and if you get caught in the middle of it, it's enough to put you off investing forever. We have seen it many times before, Black Monday of 1987, the dotcom bubble burst of 2000, the financial crash of 2007/8, the Coronavirus crash of 2020 and so on.

The question is: how does the DIP measure up when faced with such horrendous market conditions? Let's face it, no investment strategy is going to do well in these types of conditions.

Well, believe it or not, the DIP handles this extreme market crash scenario surprisingly well. Let me explain.

1. FLIGHT TO SAFETY

When the stock market crashes, the first thing that investors do is run and take cover. It's like being in a war and your enemy is dropping bombs on you from above. You are not thinking of anything else other than to get the hell out of there and seek shelter, protection and safety. Right?

It's the same with the stock market. When bad news hits the marketplace, we all want to protect what we have and the best way to do that is to find the safest location. And when it comes to investing there is no safer location than low risk, long-established companies that pay sustainable dividends. In other words, there is a mass migration of investors who move away from the higher risk companies that they might currently be holding and shift their money into lower-risk companies and funds – this movement of capital is known as 'a flight to safety'.

This movement of capital into the biggest and safest companies happens across the world, whether it's here in the UK, Europe, the

United States, or the Far East. The exact 'flight of safety' principle applies everywhere.

And the great news is that the DIP System is perfectly placed to benefit from this inflow of funds.

This doesn't mean that your shares will go up in price. In a falling market, everything is going to lose value. Perhaps with the exception of gold, you are going to see a reduction in prices globally, that's why it's called a global stock market crash. But at least with the DIP strategy, you can be assured that you will be holding those companies which are likely to suffer the *least.*

When there is a war and bombs are dropping from the sky it's unrealistic to expect there won't be any collateral damage. Of course, there will be damage and that means that your portfolio will fall in value. There is no getting away from that.

Therefore it becomes a case of risk mitigation rather than risk avoidance. It's impossible to avoid risk completely unless you either sell your entire portfolio and go into cash before the crash happens or you can use hedging strategies to neutralise your risk position. If you know what you are doing, you could even make a lot of money by shorting using derivatives and options but let's leave that discussion for another book.

Of course, if investors are so scared that the stock market will crash, they may even just sell their whole portfolios and go into bonds or cash, but that's going to be a small % of the population, maybe 5% of investors might make those kinds of radical, sweeping changes. Most investors will typically ride out the wave, knowing that the market will eventually recover. History has shown us time and time again that's what happens.

Therefore the best way to protect against a crash is to hold assets with the lowest denomination of risk. If the asset class that you are holding is equities then investments in the largest, dividend-paying companies is usually a very good start.

2. PART CASH, PART INVESTED

The DIP Strategy also has a built-in safety mechanism against a stock market crash from the way that it is designed because, throughout the year, your share portfolio will be partly in cash and partly invested. This means that in the event of a stock market crash your portfolio is only partially at risk. This is unlike most managed portfolios which are nearly always completely invested. In fact, a typical investment portfolio rarely has more than 2-3% in cash which means that when the market does crash 97-98% of it is at risk.

Because the DIP constantly forces your share portfolio to oscillate from being invested and not invested, from equities to cash, you will see that at any given moment your portfolio will typically have a healthy amount of cash waiting for the next opportunity.

The cash element has two big advantages. Firstly, it gives 100% protection against a stock market crash and secondly, and more importantly, in my opinion, it gives DIP investors the huge advantage of being able to buy shares *after* the crash at very cheap prices.

History has shown us that the biggest profits are usually made in the 6-12 month recovery period immediately following a market crash. The problem is that most investors have no money to invest at that point because they've already lost so much during the crash. Those who are holding cash put themselves in a very enviable position and the DIP helps them to do this.

3. COLLECTING INCOME

Another reason that the DIP Strategy is better equipped to deal with a market crash than your average share portfolio is that every one of your companies will be paying you a healthy dividend.

It means that if the market stays low for a year or two before it starts to recover you are still going to be generating probably somewhere between 5% and 7% per annum (depending on your risk assessment). If you can be patient and wait until the storm eventually blows over, the shares will pay you just to sit and wait.

Using the house analogy again, it's like buying a house which generates a great rental income and positive cash flow, but which has fallen in price and is in negative equity. It's not really an issue unless you plan on selling your house. But if you can afford to hold it until the housing market recovers you will be fine. So like Risk 2, when the shares fall in value, you just have to play the buy and hold game and wait for the recovery.

4. LESS RISK

We already know from the Dividend Yield Support (DYS) theory that companies which pay a dividend provide a natural level of support that isn't available to non-dividend paying shares. This support reduces the risk and impact of the fall because as the price slides investors are more likely to buy. It also reduces the rate at which the price falls.

This doesn't mean that dividend-paying companies can't go bust. Of course, any company has the potential to disappear but dividend-paying companies (which tend to be profitable and have positive cash flow), are going to be able to deal better with economic recessions, terrorist attacks, banking crises, economic lockdowns and so on. They have that extra financial buffer that is not afforded to businesses which are less profitable and therefore by definition are usually not the best dividend payers.

And if things get really bad then at least dividend-paying companies have the option to cut, suspend or even cancel their dividends completely. Each of these acts is preferable to falling into administration and more importantly they give you, the investor, the opportunity to assess and exit if necessary.

RISK 5 – SHARES FALL IN PRICE - DIVIDEND CUT

This is clearly the biggest risk of them all, and yes, it's even bigger than a stock market crash, risk 4. That's because a stock market crash won't affect the DIP strategy unless the companies cut their dividends. If companies cut their dividends, then the very foundation upon which the entire strategy is based becomes compromised. There is also a good chance that a company won't go from paying a dividend to going bust without the dividend being scrapped first. In other words, risk 5 (a dividend cut) is greatest after risk 4 (a market collapse) occurs.

If a company cuts a dividend when there isn't a market collapse, then it means that you have probably chosen your stock unwisely. A solid, blue-chip business with a reliable dividend cover shouldn't be cancelling their dividend unless the market conditions change very unfavourably against it. If it does, then this usually suggests an internal problem within the company which you didn't spot.

So let's see how the DIP copes with this risk because this really is the big one.

Imagine that you buy shares using the DIP strategy and that you are happily collecting the dividends and you're also taking profits along the way. All is going well and then suddenly and out of the blue, the company announces that it's going to reduce or even scrap the dividend. This brings a large sell-off as investors panic and the share price collapses.

This is probably the worst thing that can happen to the DIP strategy because the entire system is now defunct. All of the exit prices and entry prices mean nothing and there will be two significant impacts on the investor.

Firstly, the investor loses some or all of their future dividend payments. This means less or no income so what was supposed to be an income play has quickly become a capital growth play. That's not ideal when there is no capital growth because share prices have fallen! It also means that all of the calculations have to be redone from scratch based on the new reduced dividend payments.

Secondly, the share price is likely to fall, and potentially quite dramatically depending on how severe the dividend cut is and how badly the market reacts to the news. That's because a dividend cut is usually viewed as a last resort which means that the company may well be in deep, troubled waters.

The news could also lead to professional fund managers removing the company from their income-based funds, which would exacerbate the fall even further.

A company that used to pay a dividend but can no longer afford to becomes a ticking time bomb. The uncertainty around that company becomes so great, that nobody except the uninformed or the speculators are usually going to want to keep it.

It's like buying a house that is let to students paying high rent because it's perfectly located right next to a university. Then suddenly the university closes down and the students relocate to a new city. The income has gone, and that house falls in value. Now we have a problem, Houston.

It won't surprise you that I have thought about this problem long and hard because I knew that this would be the biggest challenge facing the DIP. But like all problems, I also knew that there had to be a solution. In fact, it turns out that there wasn't one but four solutions to this potential problem.

1. RISK ASSESSMENT

It's no coincidence that the dividend cover is the first variable in the risk assessment process – that's because it's the most important. A good dividend cover goes a long way to ensure that the company which you are thinking of buying doesn't cut its dividend. By being strict with yourself in this area, you significantly reduce the risk of

DIVIDEND INCOME PLUS - 163

being faced with a scenario where your shares have their dividends slashed.

2. MONITORING

The DIP System forces you to monitor things. The danger of buying investments and then leaving them alone as part of a 'long term' buy and hold strategy is that you don't look at them, you don't monitor them, and you leave them to manage themselves.

It's the same risk that you have when you leave your young children unattended and without supervision. It doesn't usually end well.

Your shares should be treated like your children. You want to protect and nurture them and that's why you need to pay close attention to them. The good news is that before things escalate into real problems, you can usually see the signs.

Companies will very rarely go from hero to zero. That just doesn't happen in the real world.

What is far more likely is that you will begin to see some news flow, often from the company itself, to advise shareholders of 'challenging times ahead' or 'difficult trading conditions' or similar words to watch out for.

And there isn't just one warning, but usually multiple warnings over a period, typically several months at least. There might be other signals to look out for too, such as whether directors are selling their shares, or if the company is being short-sold in the market place by professional traders, or whether the company is being forced to pay dividends from pension funds instead of out of profits, or if the Chief Financial Officer (CFO) has stepped down.

The point is that the red flags are easy to spot if you know what to look for.

If you don't know what those flags are, or you do know but you just aren't paying attention to them, then that's the source of the problem.

That's why the DIP system works so well. Because it forces you to regularly review your positions to ensure that the initial risk assessment that you did at the outset still holds true today. If the company has fundamentally shifted, if the sector is coming under pressure, if the financials are moving, if the dividend cover has dropped or even if you just have a 'bad feeling' about the company, the answer is simple – SELL.

And if you miss all those signs then you will still see it in the price. That's because even if you miss those signs the rest of the market won't. They *will* see those signs and they will push the price down and as you see that happening, you will know that your calculation is wrong. You still won't know why it's wrong, you just know that the rule of elasticity means that the shares should bounce quickly after purchase and if they don't then your calculations are wrong which means you have to recalibrate and you have to exit.

This is very different from an investor who buys a dividend-paying company for the long term and then doesn't monitor it because he makes the false assumption that the company will keep paying that dividend forever. Can you see the difference in approach? The DIP forces you to become a better and more informed investor.

The DIP means that there should be no reason for you to miss an opportunity to sell a position *before* the company cuts its dividend. Remember companies don't usually cut dividends without a lot of pressure on them to do so; it's a last resort of desperation, a sign of weakness, and something that they always want to avoid.

And that's why the DIP is so powerful. As an investor, it moves you out of that unproductive state of buy and hope for the best and moves you into that much healthier state of buying *and selling* – that's of huge psychological importance.

The DIP makes you think about the sale – either at a profit which is ideal or when necessary at a loss to mitigate the risk, which is just as important. Once you are mentally ready to sell then it changes the way you invest. Most investors focus their time and effort on buying, what to buy and when to buy.

The DIP brings the sale into your mind. Now the conversation becomes what should I buy, when should I buy it, and when should I sell? Do you see how the DIP takes a novice investor and makes them more well-rounded, more professional? And it does so without force or pressure. It just becomes naturally the sensible thing to do.

Most investors who are used to buying but not selling will be caught like deer in headlights when companies cut their dividends and their share prices fall. The DIP stops you from being a deer.

It mentally prepares you for the sale and so when you see something in your system which makes you feel uncomfortable, it's so much easier, you just pull the trigger and sell. It doesn't matter if you are making a loss because you know it's time to sell.

That's the best way to mitigate against any form of risk – sell and get out of the position.

3. A SMALLER LOSS

If you do end up selling at a loss (remember that's a sensible thing if the company is about to cut its dividend!) then the good news is that you probably will have already collected at least some dividend income before you got to that point. This will help to offset at least part of the loss. Of course, this depends on when you purchased the shares and how many dividend payments you received before the share fell in price.

But it's still part of the equation and that's another reason why the DIP helps you to make that all-important sell decision. If I am thinking about selling a £20,000 position which might lose me 10%

i.e. £2,000 but I have already collected £1,000 in dividends, then I'm more likely to sell. My net loss is only £1000 or 5% - if I'm worried that the company could cut its dividend and result in the share price falling by 20%, then selling now 5% down is a pretty easy decision.

However, if the company hadn't paid me £1,000 in dividends and there was a risk that it could fall by 20% then I might think I am already down 10%, I may as well take the gamble and see what happens.

Another big mistake of course, "let's see what happens" are the most common last words of every investor just before they went broke.

4. DIVERSIFICATION

Diversification is the final piece of the risk mitigation jigsaw because the DIP Strategy is a fund itself. This is not an individual company, it's a collection of companies.

So, let's assume that everything that could go wrong, does go wrong.

Let's say that your risk assessment was terrible, you picked a stock that you shouldn't have, the company doesn't give any pre-warning and just cuts its dividend (or it gives lots of warnings but you miss them all), and you don't even collect any dividends because you only bought the shares last week – even after all of that, diversification still allows the DIP to help you to mitigate risk.

The likelihood that all or even the majority of your companies simultaneously cut their dividends is almost impossible.

Remember that the DIP is a portfolio of companies, maybe 20 or 30 in total. Therefore, even if one of those companies cuts its dividend and falls in price, it still only has a relatively small impact on the whole strategy. And if you see that two or three companies are cutting their dividends you will probably notice that it's specific to a sector in which case you can make that judgement to exit those companies affected.

But for companies across all sectors and industries that have been paying dividends for decades, to scrap their dividends at the same time would be so improbable that you could almost rule it out. Even during this recent Coronavirus stock market crash, companies only reduced their dividends or temporarily suspended them.

The point is that even when faced with the mother of all risks, the dreaded Dividend Cut, the DIP still has a built-in mechanism which sensibly manages it.

Theory into Practice

When I began writing this book it was in 2018 but because of everything that goes on in our busy lives, what should have been a 6-month turn-around took over 2 years. That wasn't great for somebody like me who is wildly impatient, but it did have one huge benefit for readers which I wasn't expecting.

It turns out that the DIP would face its biggest challenge, not in theory but in practice.

In March 2020 and the coming months, the entire world went into lockdown to protect against the spread of the Coronavirus. This sent the stock market spiralling down into a major crash and within this period, many companies announced that they would cut their dividends. There were also many companies which were unable to withstand the lockdown and filed for bankruptcy. Two interesting things happened.

Firstly, the companies that filed for bankruptcy were, and as the DIP theory predicted, almost exclusively those listed businesses that did not pay dividends. In fact, I can't think of a single company that paid a dividend before the 2020 stock market crash which subsequently folded. That might change going forward depending on how bad this downturn becomes, but it's clear that the companies which weathered the storm the best were those which paid dividends to investors.

Secondly, a huge swathe of dividend-paying companies either cut or completely suspended their dividends. This was the biggest challenge that the DIP would face because the DIP had really come into play from 2011 onwards. Therefore, it had missed the 2008 crash and had not up until this point been fully tested with a major stock market crash.

An unprecedented 50 companies on the FTSE100 reduced their dividends in the first half of the year. A further 108 companies on the FTSE250 index did the same and 139 on the AIM market. In total, a staggering 445 companies on the London Stock Exchange either suspended or cancelled dividend payments in the first six months of 2020, and this trend is most likely going to continue.

As a result, my team and I were forced to take swift and immediate action. We adapted the DIP strategy in light of the dividend cuts and amazingly we were able to make more money for clients using the strategy in the following 3 months than we had made in the previous 12 months. The companies that were traded didn't change but the investment approach did. The elastic band analogy also still worked fine except it became a lot more elastic and the extremes were further apart. This is because companies became more difficult to price accurately and so the difference between the true and fair values stretched more than usual. This meant that the opportunity for larger profits became much greater.

Another strange phenomenon occurred which as companies announced that they were reducing or suspending their dividends, many of them jumped up in price! I watched in astonishment as I saw companies rise by as much as 10% in a single day after they announced that they were suspending their dividends! I had never seen this before but then it began to make sense to me. The market recognised the importance of prudence and recognised that those businesses that would keep their cash reserves and not pay out unnecessary dividends to shareholders, would be best protected against future lockdowns. In other words, they would be better prepared for the future. It wasn't that companies couldn't afford to pay dividends but rather it didn't make any financial sense to do so.

After all, it would be a terrible idea to appease shareholders today by making dividend payments when that could increase the risk of the company falling into trouble next year. Therefore, the reason why a company cuts a dividend is probably more important than the act itself. Most of the FTSE100 companies cut their dividends not because they had to but because it was the right thing to do for the longevity of the business. It also helped that it was the perfect time to do so as so many other firms were doing the same, which meant that shareholders understood and agreed with that decision. There's nothing worse than one firm cutting a dividend when no other firm does, but because this was a collective response to a global period of unprecedented uncertainty, dividend cuts were not only widely accepted but in fact encouraged. Shareholders saw the bigger picture.

On the one hand, the income loss was a blow, but the increased capital appreciation more than made up for that loss. If you go to the DIP website you will see many examples from March-July 2020 which show a number of trades that made substantial profits during that time. It was incredible.

Of course, the risks were higher and not every trade was a success but overall it benefitted clients. The ends of the elastic band may have been more difficult to judge because it was no longer based on dividend yields but because of the greater distance between low and high, it was easier to sit closer to the point of equilibrium and still make money. Therefore, the DIP morphed in 2020 from an income-based strategy into a short-term capital appreciation strategy but continued to use the very similar risk parameters. I'm not suggesting that this was intentional and as somebody who believes passionately in income and dividends, I look forward to 2021 and 2022 when dividends should hopefully resume in full.

However, I am also incredibly pleased that faced with the biggest risk that the DIP could have faced, it reacted as well as I could have ever imagined. The ability to shift the DIP strategy whilst maintaining so much of its core elements particularly in terms of risk assessment was the key to its success.

The Conclusion on Risk

Hopefully, I have covered the discussion of risk in a fair and unbiased manner. I am incredibly self-critical and judge myself harshly in many aspects of my life because I know that constructive criticism helps us to become the best version of ourselves. The DIP is no different.

I need to be confident that the DIP will stand up to the stress that the stock market will from time to time be obliged to put it under. This doesn't mean that the DIP isn't without risk because the concept of investing without risk is a fallacy.

The DIP does have risks like any other investment strategy but fundamentally those risks are mitigated considerably by how it is constructed. Because it combines the best elements of the three fundamental building blocks of all share portfolios i.e. income, growth and capital preservation, it is able to control the risk so much better.

Most importantly the DIP stood up to the strictest of tests, which was the suspension of dividend payments from at least 50% of companies. With some careful manoeuvring the DIP, albeit a different, more streamlined version, was able to produce the most staggering results.

I can't say whether in the next crash I will be able to do the same but it gives me great confidence in knowing that it's possible. At a time when investors were losing money, we are thankful that we could offer clients a real alternative that actually made money during these difficult times.

As it turns out the stock market rallied strongly after March due to unprecedented amounts of quantitative easing stimuli from central banks around the world, which pushed trillions of dollars into the money supply. That certainly made it easier for the DIP to make a profit, but it was the strategy itself that allowed us to fully capitalise on the opportunity and generate above-market returns. If it carries on like this, 2020 could end up being a record year for many investors, and who would have imagined that could happen during a pandemic?

And if the market does crash again, the DIP will certainly handle that fall much better than any buy and hold strategy could.

So, there you have it.

I have listed every possible risk that I can think of and I've also been very strict with those risks. I haven't watered them down or pretended that they won't happen. I've done the opposite – I've stress-tested them beyond what is likely to happen, for you and for my own peace of mind, so that I know that the DIP works. And I'm glad to say that the DIP stands strong and tall in the face of such adversity.

This doesn't mean that you won't lose money with the DIP, of course, you will. There's no strategy in the world that will make money if the stock market crashes, if thousands of multi-national companies simultaneously issue profit warnings or if there is a flu pandemic and the economy plummets into a depression. Unless you are a professional and know how to short then you're going to lose so it's just a choice of which strategy loses least. To that end, the DIP comes out on top.

And if you are an investor in the stock market then you already have risk, whether you like it or not.

Therefore, you need to consider whether the DIP strategy increases or reduces your risk, and this depends largely on the type of portfolio that you currently have.

If you have a very low-risk portfolio which includes fixed-income investments like gilts and bonds, maybe a few preference shares and some very low-risk unit trusts, well then it is fair to say that the DIP Strategy will almost certainly increase the risk because you are investing into direct, individual companies within the equity market. But with that increased risk also comes the possibility for much bigger returns.

However, if you already hold a portion of your portfolio either in individual companies or certain funds then the DIP strategy in all likelihood will probably *reduce* your overall level of risk. Obviously, this will depend on the companies and funds that you hold and their individual risk.

In any case remember that YOU control what goes in and what goes out of the DIP, and at what price. This means that you can change the risk of the strategy according to what you feel most comfortable with. In other words, you can either make the DIP Strategy low, medium or high risk according to your appetite for risk.

We already know that risk is never going to be your problem – it's understanding how to manage it effectively that will define the success of your investments.

Also, let's not forget that we haven't even discussed what might happen if the opposite to those risks happened. For example, how much more profitable would the DIP strategy be if a company instead of cutting its dividend *increased* its dividend? What if the stock market didn't crash but went up significantly? And what if the economy didn't slip into recession but started to boom and all of the major companies began to post exceptional profits? How much money could the DIP make then?

The next question to answer is whether the DIP strategy is right for you.

CHAPTER 14

IS THE DIP RIGHT FOR YOU?

In this chapter, I am going to go through the key benefits of the DIP and the types of investors that I believe that it will be particularly suitable for, and therefore helpful too. Not every strategy is suitable for every type of investor and over the next few pages, you will see whether this approach is or isn't aligned to your investment objectives.

LOW TO MEDIUM RISK

The DIP System is particularly suited to low and medium risk investors because it focusses on lower-risk investments, specifically the biggest and most profitable companies which pay sustainable dividends. Depending on which companies you choose to invest in, the risk can be tweaked from very low to very high but typically most investments fall into the bracket of 'low to medium'.

It's hard to find a very high-risk company that pays a sustainable dividend and so therefore the DIP strategy immediately eliminates by default the riskiest companies in the marketplace. That's a pretty effective filter on its own if you want to avoid any companies which are too racy.

Of course, the concept of assessing risk is subjective, and so when I say 'low' this should be seen in the context of the equity market. A 'low' risk investment, depending on who you are speaking to, could be cash or a fixed income bond like a gilt or it could even be a unit trust. Therefore 'low to medium' in the context of this book refers to the risk of <u>equities</u> and specifically direct shareholdings, rather than funds.

HIGH INCOME

The average dividend yield of a properly constructed DIP portfolio is probably between 5% and 6% which is typically twice the yield of the majority of share portfolios that I review for investors. Most portfolios that I have reviewed have an average yield of less than 3% because they have a balance of income and capital growth stocks. Therefore, only half of their portfolio provides income (and usually quite low income) whilst the other part pays no income at all.

The DIP is therefore for investors who want a consistent and reliable level of income flow. That's because the majority of the income that is generated within the financial markets comes from dividends paid out by individual companies, and the highest income occurs when you are able to buy companies at the lowest prices.

Oddly enough, products which are specifically designed to produce income (i.e. 'fixed-income' products including bonds) usually fail miserably. The income is so pitiful that any income generated is eaten up in annual fees and charges. Part of the problem is investing in Government debt like US Treasuries or UK Gilts which give an income yield of 2% or less. I understand the risk trade-off between shares and bonds but there is a tipping point where the return is so low on bonds that you almost might as well keep the cash in the bank and suffer inflation.

A sensible equity portfolio on the other hand has the potential to create significantly more income. Paradoxically, using the DIP, the asset class of equities which is not designed to give you income, actually gives you *more* income than the asset class of fixed income which is designed to give you income.

If you want income and lots of it, then the DIP System has it in abundance.

HIGHER RATE TAXPAYER

With income comes the unavoidable issue of tax, but the DIP has been constructed in such a way that it even solves this problem. That's because capital gains are taxed more favourably than income and so by converting some of your dividend income into capital appreciation you are able to reduce your tax bill.

The problem with just collecting dividends from now until forever is that you will end up paying a lot of income tax. However, the DIP portfolios that I run don't have this problem because the total performance is split between both dividends *and* capital growth.

In fact, when you are building your own DIP portfolio you should be really concerned if your total return in the year is generated solely from dividend income. If the DIP is working well, you should be getting a large number of sales being executed throughout the year. If you're not then either your entry price wasn't aggressive enough, or your sell price is too aggressive, or both.

By utilising both your income and capital gains tax allowances more effectively you are spreading the tax burden more efficiently. This is in stark contrast to the millions of investors who currently pay income tax on their share portfolios and yet each year they never even use their capital gains tax (CGT) allowance.

If you're a higher or additional-rate taxpayer, the penalties of not having sensible tax mitigation in play are even more costly than for basic-rate taxpayers, but tax is something that everybody should consider.

I have seen many investors over the years who have worked so hard to build up share portfolios and yet pay no attention to tax. There is a misguided assumption that tax is a fixed, immovable cost that has to be paid so there is no point even thinking about it.

Tax does have to be paid but some people definitely pay more tax than they need to. Reducing tax should be regarded as one of the tenets of a good investment strategy and the DIP already has that built into the system. As you go through the year and calculate your returns you can even shift the DIP ever so slightly so that it favours either income or capital growth. For example, if you haven't used your CGT allowance for the year you could drop your sell price and capture more sales, thereby triggering more capital gains. Similarly, you can time your purchase so that you buy just after the ex-dividend date. This means that you have a six-month window to capture a capital gain rather than collect a dividend payment.

Investing with a poor tax strategy is like filling a big bag with gold coins that has a hole in the bottom of it. It doesn't matter how many gold coins you work so hard to find, you're going to lose most of them unless you fix that hole.

The DIP also has another built-in deterrent to building up unnecessary profits which would be taxed more heavily in later years. I have also seen this many times where clients have accumulated capital gains profits running into tens of thousands of pounds over decades. Instead of selling and using their CGT allowance to downsize their position, they are now faced with huge, overweighted positions on individual companies and funds which put them in a poor risk management position. They are unable to navigate through market downturns because they lose one of the single most important tools for all investors – the ability to sell when they want to. If they do sell, they get clobbered with a massive tax bill. What a terrible position to be in.

RISK PROTECTION AGAINST A MARKET CRASH

The DIP strategy is very suitable for investors who are worried about a stock market crash.

We already know that unlike traditional buy and hold portfolios, the DIP strategy forces you to be in cash for periods of time. By doing so, it means that your portfolio will almost always have some element of cash in it waiting for new opportunities.

This means that if the stock market does crash, your portfolio will not suffer nearly as much as if it was fully invested in the stock market. It also means that you have free cash to take advantage of the new, cheap buying opportunities that will inevitably spring up. Of course, if you can sense the stock market direction shifting it's a much easier decision not to buy than to sell. In other words, the DIP forces you to have cash and so it's easy to decide not to buy if you feel that the market could fall. You just sit and wait to see what happens.

This is a very different proposition to an investor who is already 100% invested and now has to sell when the market is falling.

The DIP gives so much more protection. The psychology of *not buying* is easy, the psychology of *selling at a loss* is very difficult.

'Not buying' and staying in cash requires no action – you don't have to do anything. But to sell something that you are already invested in, well that requires action – it means that you have to consider how much money you are making or losing and whether now is a good time to sell or if you should wait. These are the things that go through your mind and it's the very things that the DIP strategy absolves you of.

SHORT-MEDIUM TIME FRAME

The DIP can be applied to the short, medium or long term. However, because the system is designed to give income *plus* capital appreciation the system is particularly suited to those who want their money working for them over weeks and months, rather than years.

'Short term' is, of course, another subjective term open to interpretation, but for the purposes of the DIP strategy, I would typically categorise short term as anything up to 3 months, and medium term up to a year. If you are holding a DIP position for more than a year then it means that your initial entry price was too high. This isn't really a big problem because with the DIP you are collecting larger than normal dividends, but the intention of the DIP is certainly not to hold a share for several years.

As a general rule, if I am holding a company that pays a dividend of say 5% and the price doesn't reach my target sell price within a 12-month window, I would look to sell because it means that the stock is within the equilibrium range of the elastic band. If I see that there are other better opportunities out there which I am missing, then I'm more likely to sell sooner.

EASY STEPS TO FOLLOW

The system has been specifically designed so that anybody can implement it. It's methodical and mechanical in its approach, which means that you don't need to be experienced.

It's also very intuitive and makes sense from a logical perspective. That's one of the keys to its success because when you understand something it gives you the confidence to follow it. It's very hard to put your trust into something that doesn't make sense or that is too complicated to follow.

If you try to do that you are essentially driving blind whilst listening to somebody else's instructions.

That's fine for a while, but when you eventually crash (and at some point, you will), this will damage your confidence so much that you won't want to drive again. With the DIP and over time you know that fundamentally it is based on sound principles which you can trust and rely upon, even if the road might get a little treacherous in the wet sometimes.

INDIVIDUAL SHARES

This is one of the few areas where the DIP might genuinely divide the investment community.

Some investors just love funds - they just can't get enough of their unit trusts, investment trusts and mutual funds. It doesn't matter whether those funds are underperforming, whether they are ridiculously non-transparent and expensive, if they're poorly managed, or that they have no control over what goes into or out of them. It doesn't even matter that they have so little control over them that the funds can be suspended without warning. The fact is that some investors just have an affinity for funds.

Those who favour funds usually do so either because of previous bad experiences where they have lost money in individual shares or because they don't feel that they have the knowledge to invest in direct shareholdings. It's also hard to move from funds to shares when the biggest and most powerful financial institutions in the world have such a stranglehold on funds and the narrative that goes with them which is that funds are the only way to invest. When the whole financial eco-system teaches you to love funds because share trading is too risky, it's not difficult to understand why most people now follow that advice. I also understand that funds become more attractive when there is no alternative option to consider.

But I also know that if those investors were offered a genuine alternative that could work better than their existing fund strategy, at a lower cost, and with better results, then the vast majority would be interested to hear more.

That's why the DIP Strategy is disruptive in the industry. That's a great thing. Investors finally have a real choice to consider between what really is best – funds or shares.

And if they still can't decide, well at least they now have a choice that they didn't have before.

BIG, BLUE-CHIP, SAFE COMPANIES

The DIP is particularly catered towards the biggest and best companies in the marketplace, which means that it is suited to all the major indices across the world. Therefore, if you like the idea of the most established, blue-chip companies to put your money into, then the DIP is perfect. These companies are also the safest shares in the whole of the stock market and so attract a lot of interest.

Of course, the DIP can be applied not just to the main market stocks but also to companies on the smaller exchanges that pay dividends. However, in my experience, there isn't any real need to venture into the small-cap market because the blue-chip companies will give you ample investment opportunities. Therefore, if you like the idea of investing in big companies, the DIP is more suited to you.

AUTOMATION

As you know the DIP has been designed with automation in mind. It means that you can implement it and then leave it to work. Apart from the initial risk assessment which doesn't take very long (and in any case is really the fun part once you play with the numbers), this system functions perfectly well on autopilot.

The only thing that you really need to monitor is the market news – the way to do this is to simply add alerts to your system to be notified of any company announcements that you're holding within your DIP portfolio. The announcements will allow you to keep a track of any news that might impact the dividend of the companies that you are holding (or intending to buy) and should give you ample warning to exit in the event that there is any increased risk to the future income pay-outs or to adjust the buy and sell prices where necessary.

Other than reading the market news, which won't take you more than a few minutes, the portfolio requires very little management.

So let's consider that most investors usually fall into one of two groups.

The first group spends way too much time analysing and researching their investments but usually don't have the expertise to take that information and really benefit from it. Usually, there is only a tiny net positive return from all that extra hard work which barely makes it worth their effort.

The second group of investors don't spend nearly enough time and completely neglect their portfolios and therefore almost always lose money. The second group naturally tends to move towards funds because they believe that a fund manager can do the job better than they can, and usually, they are right. However, finding somebody who happens to be better than you, when you know that you suck, is probably not the optimal solution either.

An automated system like the DIP is a happy place in between these two extremes, which gives you control, helps you to understand your investments, gives you a positive return on the time that you spend, but also automates many decisions using a formulaic approach so that it doesn't consume your life. For the hours that you put in every week or month, it gives you the best return on that investment of time.

Automation also helps to eliminate emotional factors that would otherwise cloud the decision-making process. Automation means objectivity, which in turn means confidence and more consistent results.

It also creates a built-in level of discipline which mustn't be underestimated. When it comes to investing it's clear that the most successful investors are those who are most disciplined. Being able to sell when you are losing or able to sell and take a profit when you're winning in a strict and clinical approach, isn't a skill that most of us are born with. I wasn't.

It's a skill that you have to learn and then practise over and over, until it becomes habitual. It requires discipline and can take years, even decades to master. Most people don't have the time or patience to spend years to become that good. That's where the DIP comes in – it provides an easy short cut to success by creating a set of investment rules which require minimal effort and discipline.

You just have to follow the system.

BETTER PERFORMANCE

This ultimately is what it all comes down to – better performance. In addition to all the other benefits of the DIP, the single, biggest reason that any investor would want to use it is for a better return on their investment portfolio.

The question is "Can the DIP give better than average results and if so, prove it."

Let's break it down again and recap. We know that the performance of any investment portfolio is built on three key elements, capital preservation, dividend income and capital growth, so let's look at each one in terms of why the DIP should perform better.

1 Capital Preservation – we have already seen how the DIP gives a better level of protection than individual share investing and particularly in the event of a stock market crash. Tick.

2 Income - the income obviously must be higher with the DIP strategy than a standard investment strategy, where you just buy a load of random dividend-paying shares. That's because your entry price has been especially chosen to maximise the dividend yield. Double Tick.

3 Capital Appreciation – it's easy to assess the DIP against the two most common investment strategies so let's look at each one.

a) Buy and sell trading – this is high-frequency strategy, takes a lot of time and effort, requires great expertise and involves higher trading costs. Unless you are a professional trader who is very experienced in this area and can commit several hours every day to trade in this way, this is a very difficult strategy to become successful in. Many smart people have left their full-time jobs to try and make it as 'day-traders' and most have failed.

It's not easy and certainly not appropriate for the average investor. It's not ideal because usually traders will use products such as CFDs and spreadbetting, both of which carry very high risk.

b) Buy and hold – this is what most investors already do but it has serious limitations that we have already discussed. In fact, the only time that I can think of where a buy and hold strategy might work better than the DIP is if the market is increasing at a rampant rate, for example during that very early stage at the beginning of a bull market.

However, this sharp bull recovery only takes place in a very short window, usually just for a few months immediately after a serious crash. And let's be honest – how many people are lucky enough to have the cash and the courage to invest at that exact right moment? I don't know of many.

Even when there is a bull market, the shares don't just go up in a straight line, they go up and down in an upward trading channel. That's why I have been able to use the DIP strategy just as effectively in a bull market. Remember, that after a stock market crashes by 40% then you know that the next few months will probably show incredible growth. Therefore, there is nothing stopping you from shifting the DIP strategy for that period of time by extending the selling price to capture the larger gains on offer. Once the market has gone past that initial spurt of 'explosive growth' then things will return to normality at which point you can switch back to the old DIP strategy parameters.

Remember that the buy and hold strategy only *appears* to work because the stock market goes up over the long term, but that's very dangerous because it lulls you into a false sense of security. What it doesn't show you is that you are missing the real opportunity of buying at rock bottom prices after a crash. It unfairly removes your access pass to what the stock market is really offering.

Compared to the two strategies (trading versus investing), the DIP sits proudly in the middle. It takes the best from both approaches and combines them together.

CHAPTER 15

THE DIP v BUY & HOLD

The real question comes down to whether the DIP system offers a better return to risk pay-out (and can therefore be deemed as a superior trading system) than the classic buy and hold strategy. It's about making a direct comparison between the single most popular investment strategy over the past 50 years and still used today by most private investors against the DIP.

It's about having an honest conversation regarding what is the most popular investment approach in the marketplace today and seeing whether there really is a better alternative and if there is, what that alternative might look like.

Of course, it's not about comparing the risk of the DIP strategy to the risk of having cash in the bank; clearly, that's an unfair comparison.

The DIP shouldn't be seen in isolation. It should be considered in comparison to what your current investment strategy looks like. That's why when you consider how effectively the DIP System mitigates the risks, and look at it completely objectively, I think that you should rightfully arrive at the conclusion that at least for those people to whom it is most suited (low risk, short-medium term, dividend income seekers), it offers a far superior solution to the standard buy and hold strategy.

It's about comparing two investment strategies and throwing out the old biases and outdated perceptions. It's a simple question – with all other things being equal, which one wins, and which one loses? My work, research, analysis and 20 plus years trading as a professional in the City of London, tells me that the DIP wins.

SYSTEMS AND PRACTITIONERS

Performance comes down to the trading systems and their practitioners i.e. it comes down to the vehicles and those who drive them. Therefore, the system needs to work, but the person operating it must also know what he or she is doing. You can make a great living from both short-term trading and a buy and hold investment approach, but you need to know what you're doing in both cases.

But to bring them together is something that hasn't really been fully explored before. I believe that the DIP strategy takes the best from both conventional approaches and offers a more complete solution.

Of course, I am never going to give any assurances on performance and it's not for me to say how the system that I have created might perform for you.

For me personally, and for my clients, I can just say this - it's one of the best investment systems that I have ever used. Will it stand up to scrutiny 10, 20 or 30 years from now?

I believe that it will. That's because the concept of a falling asset price increasing yield is timeless. That principle will never change, not now, not tomorrow, not ever.

IMPROVING PERFORMANCE BY TAKING A LOSS

Not every trade is always going to win and so as an investor, I want to remind you that it's okay to take a loss.

In fact, it's healthy to take a loss from time to time. It shows that you are not infallible, it keeps you on your toes and it ensures that you remain humble.

In my experience, and having reviewed literally thousands of share portfolios over the years, from absolute beginner investors to seasoned professionals, one of the primary reasons that people don't make as much money in the stock market as they should is this – they don't sell when things go bad.

That's it. It's not the profitable positions that let people down. It's the losing positions that do that. That's because most investors follow the same, trodden, worn-out path – the investment mantra of the entire world it seems is "*I am a buy and hold investor, I will hold those shares forever if I have to, I buy for income so I don't care about the share price, they will come good eventually*' – blah, blah, blah.

No, actually they probably won't 'come good' eventually. The companies that fall because of a profits warning or a cut in their dividends or because the sector is out of favour very rarely go back up in price, and if they do, there is so much pain that one must endure that it just isn't worth it. It is far more sensible to take a relatively small loss and move on.

The DIP allows you to do this. You need to be sensible and take losses whenever necessary.

It's like taking care of your garden. Every so often you need to take out the weeds and if you don't then the weeds will ruin the flowers. Identify those weeds, monitor them closely and when necessary pull that little BLEEP out – that's how you need to treat your losses.

Even companies that were doing great when you first analysed them will usually over time lose their way and if that's the case, then it's okay to sell. Just because you bought a great company two years ago doesn't mean that it's the same great company today, in fact, it's probably a very different company.

The DIP is powerful because it's unlikely for you to be in a position for too long which means that the company is unlikely to have changed too much since you purchased it. But if you were invested in certain companies for several years, then it's more likely that those companies will change over that period of time, sometimes for the better but usually for the worse. That's because companies which perform well and make lots of money, will attract competitors and so their advantage quickly diminishes over time. With disruptive technologies, the marketplace is changing more quickly now than ever before. This means that the average shelf life of companies holding a number one spot in their industry is shorter now than in previous years.

With a few exceptions like Amazon and Apple, most companies will have a good run for a short period of time and then quickly fall behind. The speed at which businesses must evolve is faster than ever before and this all circles back to the idea of taking your profits when you can and not holding positions for longer than you have to.

The majority of underperforming investment portfolios have a majority of winning positions making a reasonable profit but a small number of losing positions making a huge loss. Those small number of losers have a disproportionately large impact on the performance of the entire portfolio. And this would have been completely avoidable if only there was a sensible exit strategy in place.

With the DIP there is a risk-based approach to mitigate this downside.

With the DIP you are always ready to sell, ready to recalibrate, ready to exit, ready to take action. That means no big losses in your portfolio and no weeds in your garden.

A GREAT EQUALISER

The great thing about a system like the DIP is that it's a great equaliser – it evens things up by filling in the knowledge gap which currently exists between professional investors and retail investors.

That's because most people just don't understand how the stock market works, they don't understand how companies are valued. It's not because they are not smart or intelligent, it's because they are looking at the wrong data. They look at balance sheets and profit and loss accounts but have no idea how this relates to a share price. Imagine I told you that a company generates £10m in profit per year, has £3m of debt, pays a dividend of 4% per annum and has a market capitalisation of £823m.

Now I tell you that the share price could either be 10p, 100p, 1200p or 4100p which one do you think might be the correct answer? Answer – you don't know.

What if I was to tell you that there were 17m shares in issuance? Would that help you? Yes, it would help but it still wouldn't tell you what the fair value of the price is. The point is there are too many variables and too many unknowns. For a start, the data is already old because you're relying on balance sheet information which was published maybe 6 months ago or more. Even with 'up to date' earnings reports there is always a time lag involved.

And what about things like goodwill and branding or intellectual property rights and other intangibles? How do you price that into the formula?

We can't all become accountants overnight with the ability to strip down a company's accounts and calculate fair value. Even if we could that's only going to give half of the picture.

That's why you need to look at human emotions and see what people are doing – what are their buying and selling habits, how is that affecting the share price? That's what the DIP does – it provides a short cut inroad so that you can compete in a different way, from a different perspective. There's no point in trying to run the London marathon and expect to beat the Kenyan favourite who won the race last year. But if you can take a short cut and run say 5 miles to his 26 miles, then you have a pretty good chance of beating him (unfortunately that's cheating). The good news is that you're not running a marathon, you're investing and when it comes to investing, taking a short cut isn't cheating, it's being smart.

As I have said several times already, this doesn't mean that the DIP system will always get it right. I don't always get it right either and neither will you. But that's completely okay. We should all expect losses and embrace them just in the same way that we should embrace sensibly managed risk.

If I didn't make losses, I would be more worried because that would mean my system is lucky. And if there's one thing that I don't believe in, it's luck. I don't want to be lucky, because eventually, my luck will run out and then I won't have anything.

There will be times where you might go through a bad spell of missed opportunities, trades, even a succession of losses. But the principles that support the system are and always will be sound. The concept of the Dividend Yield Support (DYS) is real – there's no getting away from it.

It's mathematics. The numbers never lie.

If you correctly calculate the initial risk assessment, and in the absence of any major catastrophe then the rest should work. Even in a catastrophe, you are going to get clobbered anyway, at least with the DIP you get clobbered less.

The DIP system is like a car. A car doesn't crash on its own – it's the driver who is responsible for the outcome. That's the same for any system and for any vehicle. There are many good trading systems just in the same way that there are many good cars on the road which will take you to your destination.

Some might be faster than others, some might be more fun, some might be tested and proven, some might be risky and dangerous.

What I have built is a Volvo – safe and reliable, but not particularly exciting.

There are many Ferraris on the road in the form of high-risk derivatives, but that's not sensible to drive especially if you don't know what you're doing.

That's why I built the DIP – for the everyday average investor. Trading is a skill and like any skill, it can be learned and over time, mastered. A good system simply helps you to accelerate that learning process ten-fold.

The professionals already have a wealth of tools and systems at their disposal, but the private investor doesn't. With the DIP now everybody has a reliable car that they can drive.

CHAPTER 16

HOW DOES THE DIP SOLVE THE PROBLEM?

At the start of this book I explained the motivation and need to create a strategy that would allow me to build my new, FCA regulated stockbroker business and compete with the numerous CFD firms in the market.

Now that you know the DIP, we can see how the DIP solved those problems. You will see how the DIP was able to replicate nearly all of the benefits that CFDs offered but *without* the associated risks. It's ground-breaking because nobody else thought of it and if they had they would be here today to tell their story.

They're not around anymore because they didn't survive, and my firm did. In fact, out of maybe 50 or more CFD brokers in the City a decade ago, you can probably count on one hand the number of CFD brokers still in operation today in London. The rest just don't exist. Two of those firms are the very large and well-established businesses IG Group and CMC Markets.

And it's because my competition has all but disappeared that I'm prepared to share my formulae with the world. Don't get me wrong, I still have a lot of competition but the smaller firms in my space are not a direct threat anymore because my business has a good brand now, it's been around for a few years and we're out of that new start-up risk stage. Besides my competition has always been with the bigger firms like St. James's Place, Hargreaves Lansdowne, Fisher Investments and so on and they're already billion-pound companies, so I'm not concerned. I'm not sure if they could use the DIP even if they wanted to, given that they operate a fund management business model.

So, let's break down how the DIP helped me to survive and then thrive when nearly all of my competitors were blown out of the water and have since disappeared.

INCREASE FUNDS UNDER MANAGEMENT VIA LEVERAGE

The first thing that CFDs allowed stockbroker firms to do was to artificially increase the funds under management through leverage. However, I knew that leverage could only be introduced by *increasing risk* and that wasn't something that I was willing to do.

Leverage is a double-edged sword. Yes, it increases the funds under management which helps to boost commissions, but that is a very short-sighted measure. CFD trades typically are not held for longer than a few days or weeks and it's impossible to really judge market direction over such a short period of time so the risk of the trade going wrong is already high. Adding leverage to that high-risk trade can be and usually is disastrous.

If the share price drops by more than a few percentage points, the CFD position has to be closed or the account is subject to a 'margin call' which means that the client is required to add further funds to keep the position open. Therefore, leverage really didn't appeal to me and it was fundamentally the thing that I wanted to avoid with the CFD model. Of course, the hard-core CFD brokers didn't care about margin calls or positions being closed out prematurely, because it meant more commission for them. They didn't care about their clients, because they had a team of 50 salespeople on the phone pressuring the next unsuspecting victim into their game to replace the one that they had just lost.

So, this was my first big challenge. How do I replace something as powerful as leverage? How could I create the same impact but without increasing the risk?

I quickly realised that I could only compensate the most powerful element of the CFD trading strategy with something just as powerful – and the only thing that I could think of in the financial markets was <u>compound interest</u>.

I knew that if I could make even a small profit on an investment portfolio but reinvest that profit and then repeat the process, I could begin to *compound* the returns. And then it dawned on me. Compound interest *is* a type of leverage. I just had to look at it differently.

Leverage is the expansion of something so that the impact is multiplied. It's like using a car jack to lift up a car by applying pressure far away from the pivot point. In other words, you are multiplying the pressure applied through leverage. Well, compound interest works in the same way except it's more gradual and discreet, but the long-term impact is the same.

If I make a decent amount of capital growth and dividend income through the DIP strategy, take none of it out and then pile it all back into the strategy plus the initial investment, and then repeat the process a few times, the capital base will increase slowly, to begin with, but then more and more quickly, i.e. it will multiply.

The only difference between my method of multiplication (compound interest) and the CFD firms' method of multiplication would be time – my approach could take years whereas the CFD method is instantaneous.

A CFD account worth £10,000 would be worth £100,000 on day one through leverage. For me to turn £10,000 into £100,000 could take years. However, I had one big advantage on my side which CFD firms didn't. I didn't suffer from the *negative* multiplication impact of leverage.

If my strategy lost 10% my clients would lose £1,000 on a £10,000 account. If the CFD firm lost 10% the client would lose their entire £10,000! In other words, leverage can work for or against the firm. If the trades of the CFD firms worked they would accelerate ahead but if they didn't work, I would quickly catch up because as my portfolios gradually increased, their portfolios rapidly declined.

I know this because during that time I spoke to a lot of clients who had experience in trading CFDs and there was not a single investor that I can recall who actually made any money. It was only many years later that the FCA made it compulsory for CFD firms to publish performance numbers on the home page of their website. On average you will find that approximately 80% or more of retail investors lose money in CFDs.

It's the classic tortoise and hare race. I just knew that my approach was better for me and for my clients. I just had to be patient and concentrate on delivering results.

INCREASE FUNDS UNDER MANAGEMENT VIA MAGIC LEVERAGE (PART 2)

Compound interest is great but compared to CFD firms it was still painfully slow. Whilst it certainly provided a form of leverage it wasn't the explosive leverage that CFD firms could apply to their accounts. I couldn't just multiply a £10,000 account to £100,000. Or could I?

Well, this might surprise you, but the DIP actually solved this problem for me as well even though I wasn't expecting it at all. That's because when investors began to see the returns that they were making and realised that it was potentially high return but *without* high risk, it didn't take too long before they were keen to invest more. You see as a new business owner I was still very much learning on the job and didn't realise that the best form of leverage was from the clients themselves.

Clients don't trust financial firms with their life savings from day one. Instead, they give maybe 10% or 20% of their total wealth, to begin with and if they see good results, it's only then that they trust firms with more of their hard-earned cash. So, without expecting it I soon began to see £10,000 accounts become £100,000 accounts or even £200,000 accounts. This wasn't leverage, this was pure magic.

One day I would come to work and find a £50,000 account that I had been managing using the DIP strategy for say 3 months and which had maybe generated say £5,000 (a 10% profit), had suddenly turned into £205,000. The client had just deposited another £150,000!

The funniest thing I remember thinking during those incredible times was that I didn't even know that the client had that much money sitting in his bank account. It was as if by magic, the firm's funds under management would multiply and best of all without any gearing risk to the client.

Even though I had conducted Know Your Client (KYC) questionnaires, most clients, especially the richest ones, don't always disclose their true full financial capability and usually hold something back. There are many times where a client would 'find' another £100,000 or £200,000 that they had conveniently not told me about. Of course, it made perfect sense. They didn't trust me at the beginning and so only wanted to trial the system with a small amount of funds.

At the same time, investors would only invest small amounts of money with CFD firms because of the higher risks. And the CFD firms made the mistake of accepting those small amounts. A lot of firms accepted just £1,000! My firm, on the other hand, could do nothing with £1,000 and so we always had to start off with minimum portfolio sizes of at least £10,000 which quickly rose to £30,000, then £50,000 and above. Also, investors don't usually want to split up ISAs or SIPPs and so clients would generally either invest nothing with us or their entire portfolio. And the more that the DIP made them, the more that they invested.

Suddenly the DIP gave me a new form of leverage which the CFD firms didn't have access to. I call it *Magic Leverage* such was the power that it gave my business. It helped me not only to compete with CFD firms but to even dominate the space.

HIGH COMMISSION VIA HIGH-FREQUENCY TRADING

The other huge benefit of CFD trading which benefitted the brokers was a very high frequency of trading. This was great for the firm because of high commissions but the commission had to come from somewhere – either from the stock market or from the client account. This means that even if both my firm and the CFD firms held exactly the same amount of exposure in the market place, the CFD firms would always make much more revenue simply because of the frequency of trades. If we both had £1m of exposure they could turn that over two or three times in a week, whereas I could only turn it over maybe once in every 12 months, subject to price movement. Their commissions were therefore much greater than what I could possibly generate.

However, the DIP also fixed this problem for me.

I realised that I couldn't just follow a standard buy and hold strategy. That would be terrible for the commission because I would make a commission on the initial share purchase and nothing else. My business wouldn't last for more than a few months because once the money was invested, I couldn't generate any more revenue from sales and subsequent new purchases.

It would also be equally terrible for the client because if all I did was buy some shares and then hold them for a few years, well the client could do that on his own. In fact, he would be better off without me if he just opened an execution-only account with a cheap online broker.

The only reason that my clients used my firm was that they wanted an investment strategy that could potentially make them *more* money than they could make on their own. Equally, clients didn't want me to trade just for the sake of maximising commission in the way that many CFD firms operated.

I knew that I had to find something which sat in the middle. In other words, I needed a strategy which would be a higher frequency trading than your average buy and hold share portfolio but a lower frequency trading strategy than the CFD model which was mainly day-trading.

The DIP fitted the bill perfectly because it combined dividend income with capital appreciation. The income ensured that the clients would constantly receive some return even during bad times whilst the capital appreciation would help clients to crystallise a profit without the need to hold a stock for years, which in turn allowed the firm to capture a commission and free up funds for new investment opportunities. It was a win-win.

In fact, it was perfectly aligned. If I did my DIP calculations poorly, I would be more likely to get stuck into holding a position for longer than I had intended. Whilst the client would continue to enjoy regular dividends, I wouldn't enjoy regular commissions because I couldn't sell the position. However, if I did my DIP calculations correctly then I could pick shares which snapped back in price quickly thereby generating a healthy profit for the client over a short period of time and at the same time I would enjoy a sale commission for my efforts.

The effectiveness of the DIP became a direct barometer for the success of my clients and therefore my success.

That's why I worked so hard on refining and improving it and as I did, I became better with my risk assessment and my timing which resulted in a higher frequency of profits for the client and a higher frequency of trading commission for me.

The commissions could of course never rival CFD trading but that was okay because my commission wasn't being generated from the client account. The commission that I was receiving was being paid out from the stock market. That made a huge difference because it meant that client accounts wouldn't deplete. In fact, I made a point of never selling at a loss unless under very exceptional circumstances where I felt that the possibility of further losses was significant. Otherwise, I was prepared to suck it up and accept that it was my fault for not doing my DIP calculations correctly. I didn't want my clients to suffer so I would take the suffering on myself.

This is the exact opposite of CFD trading which is based on using tight stop-loss orders designed to be triggered regularly. This means that commissions for CFD trades come straight out of the client account, which means that the overall funds under management are constantly being depleted.

With the DIP strategy, the funds under management and the firm's revenue continued to increase.

LACK OF RESEARCH

Any investment product has the potential to make money because ultimately it comes down to picking the right shares or funds at the right time i.e. it comes down to good research. However, research is only useful if there is an incentive big enough to drive it.

The DIP was able to beat CFDs in this department with no problem at all because it was built with the right intention, to make money for the client.

Because of my knowledge of what went on behind the scenes of CFD firms, I knew that the investment advisors who were responsible for managing client accounts already expected to lose before they began trading. That's right – they *expected* to lose money.

The time and effort required by an investment advisor to research the stock market and pick winning trades outweighed the benefits in doing so. CFD firms prioritised commission targets above and beyond the priority of generating wealth for clients, therefore there was no real incentive to spend time on research and analysis. And because most of their clients started off with relatively small accounts of between £1,000 and £10,000, they were relatively easily dispensable. They could be replaced quickly when things went wrong.

An advisor knew that his job was just to generate a commission as quickly as possible and that if he lost his client, he would receive a replacement the next day. In fact, CFD firms would usually *reward* advisors who generated the most amount of commission by giving them *more* clients. So, it became a race to the bottom, who could generate the most amount of commission in the shortest period of time.

My firm did the exact opposite. In fact, one of the key metrics that I looked at when I remunerated the investment advisors who worked for me couldn't be more different. I didn't pay attention to commission but instead looked at the portfolio value itself. If the portfolio value increased, I would reward the advisor with more clients and if it decreased, they would be penalised with fewer clients.

The firm's objective was simple - to increase funds under management by delivering profitable trades. That required the very best research and analysis.

I even introduced measures which heavily penalised advisors if they lost money for clients because they didn't spend the time researching investments properly. Losing money for clients would mean financial penalties for them personally which encouraged all of my investment team to really think carefully before they picked a stock or fund.

The extra research and analysis that we spent gave my firm a huge advantage over CFD trading and it was the DIP that set the moral code for it all to happen.

In summary, the DIP helped to frame the entire ethos and culture of the company around portfolio performance. From these strong foundations, I was able to create a team whose sole purpose was to always strive towards excellent performance.

INCOME TO REPLACE CAPITAL APPRECIATION

CFDs relied heavily, almost exclusively on capital appreciation. That's because the holding period for CFDs is too small to really take advantage of dividends and so I knew that this was another opportunity for me to exploit. That's why when I was building the DIP system I knew that I had to try and really take advantage of the income element. The fact that I was able to combine all 3 elements of the investing circle (capital protection, income and capital growth) wasn't anticipated but the protection turned out to be the cherry on the cake.

The CFDs lacked **income** and so they could never compete in the long run if I was able to bring dividends into the core of the system that I would build. It seemed crazy to me that investment firms would intentionally ignore one of the most powerful elements of investing. You only had to pick up any book on share investing written in the past 50 years and you would see the power of income and dividends highlighted in bold. Therefore I knew that income would have to play a central role in my system.

All things being equal, I had the advantage of holding stocks for dividends whilst CFD firms couldn't do that. Because of the leverage, they needed to be in and out quickly. Therefore, if a stock price didn't move by much I could sit back and collect income from dividend payments whilst they couldn't. This meant that I didn't have to force capital appreciation when it wasn't forthcoming. CFD firms couldn't do that, they would have to sell prematurely and because of that they also couldn't take full advantage of the power of compound interest.

The DIP system didn't rely on single high-risk capital growth bets. Instead, it was able to replace the higher risk capital growth bets by incorporating lower risk plays in capital growth *and* income.

SHORT-TERM TRADING

CFDs had the advantage of being nimble, which meant that in very volatile market conditions, a client could be in and out of a stock very quickly. I knew that all things being equal, CFDs had a significant advantage over equities for short-term trading. This was something that share dealing couldn't really compete with and so it took me a while to figure out how the DIP could compensate for this deficiency.

CFD firms could be in and out of a stock within a day or two, and sometimes even within an hour or even a few minutes. This ability to generate lightning-quick profits and commissions was something that I couldn't compete with because this was a case of brilliant product design. It's like having a reliable Volvo and understanding that you could never beat a Ferrari in a race.

I couldn't compete against a Ferrari using a Volvo any more than I could compete against CFDs using equities. Even if I could make a profit so quickly it wouldn't be compliant if I turned over a position in a day. Besides I had other disadvantages including higher commission costs and stamp duty fees to consider.

CFDs could also get away with charging its clients *half* of the commission that equity trading would cost, simply because CFD accounts were leveraged up to their eyeballs. That was a big part of the pitch from CFD firms – they would tell their punters that their commission rates were just 0.5% instead of 1%. What they didn't tell their clients was that the *total* commission paid would be ten times as much due to 20 times as much leverage!

CFDs could also trade without any stamp duty costs saving 0.5% on purchases. This meant that a CFD trade would cost a total of 1% (0.5% to buy and sell) compared to an equity trade costing 2.5% (1% to buy and sell, 0.5% stamp duty). This allowed the CFD firm to have a lower break-even point which meant that CFD firms could exit positions sooner.

Think of the fact that 2.5% is 2 and half times more than 1% - that's a huge difference. Therefore, CFDs had a huge advantage from a product design perspective.

After many failed attempts I realised that there was just no obvious fix to this problem. I decided that I would try and compensate for this deficiency elsewhere. I knew that if CFDs could beat equities in the short term then perhaps equities might hold an unfair advantage over CFDs in the long term. If that was true I just had to discover that marginal advantage and then capitalise on it.

If my Volvo couldn't beat a Ferrari over a ¼ mile sprint, that's not to say that I couldn't beat the Ferrari over a 500-mile round-trip over badly damaged, pot-holed roads.

CFD firms had the advantage of being very nimble and so they could jump in and out of trades very quickly, but I recognised that this came at a cost; it meant that they could only generate very small returns. You can't hold a position for an hour and expect to make 20% profit so most CFD trades would make no more than 2% or 3% at the most. Equity trading on the other hand could make a total return of maybe 10-20% in a 3-month window, especially taking into account the accumulation of dividends.

Therefore, I would need only one well-researched investment idea to generate my client 20% and a CFD firm would need the equivalent of 10 trades each generating 3% (2% net after charges) to get the same return for the investor.

Executing transactions costs money and time and so one trade which generated a 20% profit for my client was significantly better than 10 trades with each CFD trade generating just 2%. The administration and running costs including risk management and compliance to manage 10 trading positions was very cost ineffective for CFD firms. However the biggest cost was the time taken by an investment advisor who had to make 10 separate telephone calls to the client to convince them before executing each trade. The likelihood of any advisor making 10 consecutive winning trades was unlikely. Therefore, in order for a CFD firm to generate a 20% profit by making net 2% returns it probably would need to execute at least 30 trades or more because some of the trades would inevitably be losers.

RETURN TO RISK RATIO

The short-term advantages of CFDs where small profits were taken violated one of the fundamental laws of investing which is to let your profits run. This meant that the return to risk ratio was violated which in turn spelled the end for the entire CFD trading model.

CFD trading makes a mockery of the return to risk ratio because an overly heightened focus on short-term trading means that profits never get beyond a few percentage points. That's why CFDs were doomed to fail.

The DIP was designed to optimise the return to risk ratio by ensuring that the differential between what an investor could earn and what they were prepared to lose was as far apart as possible. With CFDs, investors were making 3% returns, giving a net return of 2% but at the same time would have stop losses at 2% giving a net loss of 3%. That's crazy because it meant that an investor would make 2% on winning trades and lose 3% on losing trades, so they would have an inverted return to risk ratio!

With the DIP the returns that we would typically target might be say 20% with a risk of 10% which meant a 2 to 1 return to risk ratio. With dividend income, we could sometimes push that out as far as 3 to 1. This meant that we could win even just 50% of our trades whereas CFD firms had to win significantly more trades than they lost. That put them under a huge pressure to which of course they all eventually succumbed.

SHORTING

One of the biggest benefits of CFDs is to **short** the market, in other words, to sell a company *first* with the intention of buying it back at a lower price later. On face value, this was another huge advantage that CFDs held over equities because it meant that the CFD firms could make money in both a falling as well as a rising market. This meant that CFDs could make money if the market fell and make money if the market went up. Equities, on the other hand, could only make money if the market went up. Now that was another serious mountain of a problem for me to climb.

It was like trying to become heavyweight boxing champion of the world except you had to fight with one hand tied behind your back. Hardly a fair fight.

The equity market is very one-dimensional, it's just a straight, left jab. The CFD market allows you to use a jab and a solid, right cross. Clearly, a huge advantage for CFDs.

I thought about this issue long and hard for at least a few weeks during the early development stages of the DIP because I thought that there had to be something that I could do. After quite a bit of financial soul-searching, I came to the unfortunate conclusion that there really wasn't. I had to accept that it was impossible to replicate the shorting aspect. It was a tough problem because it was simply a product deficiency. There's nothing you can do about design faults on products that you didn't design.

It was like the Volvo didn't have a reverse gear but the Ferrari did. Equities can only ever make money in one direction (up), whereas CFDs could make money in two directions (up and down).

This meant that I only had access to the stock market on average just 50% of the time. If we assume that the market goes up and down for equal periods of time, then this means that equity investing probably works for half of the time, i.e. when the market goes up. The other 50% of the time when the market goes down is where equities can't make money but CFDs can.

I then set to work as to how I could potentially reduce that 50% of missed opportunity. Clearly, I couldn't stop the market from falling but I then realised that I could do something else which was almost as powerful. I realised that I could use the downward momentum from which I wasn't able to benefit because I wasn't able

208 - HOW DOES THE DIP SOLVE THE PROBLEM?

to short and turn that into a big financial benefit after the reversal. It's only because I became fascinated with how to make money from falling prices that I spotted the pattern which showed that the greatest acceleration in a price increase took place immediately after the tail end of the downward trend.

Bingo. Whilst I couldn't make money on the way down, I could use the downward movement to my advantage. The bigger and deeper the fall, the bigger and stronger the reversal. This meant that I just had to find a way to know when to buy and when that reversal would be most likely to take place.

That's where the elastic band idea really came into play. I also used this principle to guide me through when to sell.

By selling at the highest price and at the most extreme point of the elasticity curve, I could ensure that I wouldn't have to wait for too long in falling market conditions because the price would snap back down more quickly. This meant that I wouldn't have to stay in cash for too long if I could time the sale so it was close to the top of the trading range. By doing so I could reduce the window of time that I would have been excluded from the market because of falling prices, from 50% to say just 20% or maybe even 10% or less.

I began to realise that the smart strategy was to avoid being caught in the centre of the price movement of a stock, where the elastic band was close to equilibrium. Even though a stock might fall for say 3 months from its peak before it began to recover again, I recognised that most of that time, maybe 2 or even 2 ½ months out of a total of 3 months would be during the equilibrium point of that cycle, at the centre of that fall. This meant that if I could avoid that window, I could just concentrate on other investment opportunities.

The fact that the market was falling didn't have to impact my performance. As long as I wasn't holding a position during a falling market, I could hold cash instead. Whilst I couldn't make any money with the cash, I could make *more money over a shorter period of time* if I waited for longer before I purchased. In other words, I could use the falling prices to my advantage.

I didn't care about having mediocre investment opportunities in the 'flat' areas i.e. the middle of the elastic band. Shares were just as likely to go up as they were to go down during that central region and so why should I care about having those types of opportunities? What was infinitely more important was to have the opportunity to trade on the ends of the spectrum, at the extremes of the elastic band.

Somewhat surprisingly I was able to figure out a way, albeit indirectly, to take advantage of falling prices which was something that equity investors had widely regarded as impossible. The unique privilege of being able to benefit from falling prices which had been enjoyed exclusively for CFD firms for so long was now open to equity investors. And the DIP allowed me to take full advantage of it.

VOLATILITY

CFDs have the ability to amplify volatility through leverage but equities don't have leverage and so are unable to create volatility in the same way. For example, if I have an equity investment of £10,000 in company ABC then an equivalent CFD position in company ABC would be £100,000 (using leverage of 10-1). If the stock goes up by 2%, the equity position increases by 2% but the CFD position increases by 20% based on the original investment of £10,000. This means that CFD stocks are inherently more volatile which enables them to be traded in and out more frequently and for smaller profits. If company ABC goes up by just 0.5% that would mean a 5% increase in the value of the CFD account.

At a time when volatility was also increasing in the marketplace through more derivate trading and generally more uncertain market conditions, I recognised that volatility was a great opportunity which I wasn't able to exploit, which was another drawback for me and my clients.

Basically, volatility puts all the profits on turbo-boost. However, it's a double-edged sword of course which means that it also puts all of the losses on turbo-boost too.

So, I got thinking about how I could replicate volatility from CFDs but without the leverage and I found the answer once again in the elastic band concept.

By now I understood very clearly that the fastest movement in a share price was concentrated in those uncomfortable regions within the share price movement, at the *ends* of the range. This is where the price acceleration was greatest. I also understood that price acceleration is measured as to how quickly an investor can make money, and therefore could be viewed as a viable alternative for volatility. After all, they both achieved the same result, they gave investors an opportunity to make money over the shortest period of time.

Once again, I was guided towards the importance of only trading in these tails for maximum performance – by doing so I would be able to achieve instant volatility for my investors.

SUMMARY

In summary my knowledge and experience in CFD trading meant that I was already fully aware of the most powerful aspects which I had to mirror, as well as the dangers that I had to avoid.

But I was also lucky enough to have another distinct advantage. I was able to have a clear perspective from both the client and business perspective and was therefore able to combine our desired outcomes into a single strategy. Fortunately, I did not succumb to the attraction of a highly lucrative but short-term business approach which would have ultimately ended in financial ruin for me and my clients.

Instead, I took the CFD model that so many of my competitors had used and abused and built my own version, which was equally as powerful but with infinitely better results for my clients and for me. I'm very proud of that achievement.

Of course, I'm only showing you a small part of the entire journey and there were many more issues and challenges which I faced along the way. It wasn't all plain sailing. I won some of those battles and lost others, but thankfully I was able to complete the journey with great satisfaction and success.

After the journey of the DIP began, it would take at least another ten years before the game was finally up for CFD firms as the regulators stepped in and closed down the reckless party. During that decade I quietly worked away on my Volvo in the workshop away from prying eyes. I was able to design, build, innovate and improve a system that many people probably would not have thought was possible. I continued to test it during different conditions and stress-test it, and with each step, I improved it a little more than the year before.

I'm most satisfied that when I meticulously stripped away the risks of CFDs I was one step closer to removing elements which I knew could potentially hurt investors. At the same time, I remained in awe of the power and beauty of the Ferrari and so I did everything in my power to harness all that was great about CFDs into my new design. I decided that I would create a better version of the Ferrari, but one that could never be ruined by the driver. I would create a system that would be available for all, and could never be sabotaged.

Most importantly of all the DIP allowed me to reduce risks and simultaneously improve overall returns for my investors.

It wasn't perfect but it was the perfect solution to a puzzle that no other firm was able to solve.

CHAPTER 17

TESTIMONIALS

We're nearly at the end now so in this chapter you will be glad to know that I'm going to shut up and stop talking and instead I'm going to share with you the words of my own clients who have invested using the DIP strategy. I have many more testimonials just like these but hopefully, it gives a flavour of why I felt it necessary to write a book on an investment strategy.

It's quite possible that your thoughts on the DIP strategy will be shaped more by what you're about to hear in these next few pages than anything else that you have already read in this book. That's because these are testaments of people who are in exactly your shoes. These are the words of investors who share the same concerns and worries that you do. These are the individuals who share the same goals and dreams as you do.

"I was previously following a different investment strategy which was not doing that well. Then I was introduced to the Dividend Income Plus Strategy by my advisors and in less than four months it has completely transformed things.

If the performance continues like this I am seriously going to consider transferring the Halifax Stocks and Shares ISAs for me and my wife."

J Blackburn, Cambridge

"I have been using the DIP strategy for several months and thus far the results have been really good despite the stock market being lower than when we first started. I'm also worried about a stock market crash and so this is the perfect way to maintain some cash whilst still making the rest of the money work for me. So far I have made some good profits on Sainsbury's, Hikma, IMI, Lloyds, Taylor Wimpey, Tesco and others, averaging around 7-10% profit in a 2-3 month period.

Mind you it's not all been plain sailing and I am holding TalkTalk which is down by about 11% but I'm not worried because the investment manager is monitoring it closely. If it goes much lower we will be selling but that's really the only one that hasn't worked.

I was shocked to find that my biggest winner has been Centrica. I would never have bought that share myself but the DIP gives you the confidence because it follows a system. Centrica is currently making 16% profit plus a dividend of over £1,000 but my investment manager has said that we should only sell if it reaches 20%. That's comforting for me to know because everything is clear.

The great thing about this strategy is that you don't hold onto things for too long so your risk is constantly being cut every time you sell. I wouldn't be happy buying and holding anything in the market right now but just sitting in cash and earning nothing is also something which doesn't appeal to me so the DIP is perfect for me.

Overall I'm very happy with the way it's going and it's a very encouraging strategy."

M Cook, Studley

"In the first few months of using the DIP strategy, I made 30% profit in Kier Group in just one month, 11% in ITV in 6 weeks and 15% in Dixons in just 3 weeks. I didn't collect any dividends but when you make that kind of money who cares about the income! Of course, they can't all make that kind of money and a few of the shares have gone down in value but not by much and because they are low risk and I'm making more than 5% on the dividends, I'm very happy to hold."

W Hadley, St Ives

"I did a lot of research on London Stone Securities but couldn't find anything online so in the end and after a few phone calls, I took the plunge. It's too early to say about the long-term results but I can tell you that one of their first trades made me 30% in less than a month, a £5k profit! I am happy to give a testimonial because they have done a great job for me so far and they are definitely not a scam. You hear a lot about companies ripping people off and so I was really cautious. If you want an honest and fair stockbroking firm to use, I would absolutely recommend them."

K Hanson, Todmorden

There are many more examples that I can give you of clients who have similar experiences of using the DIP strategy. However, most of my clients don't really care too much about the strategy at all. They have entrusted me to manage their wealth and to implement the strategy that I feel is most appropriate for them. Therefore, they don't even know about the DIP. All that they know and quite frankly, all that they care about is for their portfolio to grow. And that's perfectly fine.

When I take my car in for a service or to fix a repair, I never ask the mechanic to go into any great detail about the tools or equipment that he's using, or the specific approach that he takes. I recognise that he is the expert and unless I have a particular desire to learn about engineering, which I don't, all that I care about is that my car is fixed. How he does it is really up to him.

It's the same with investing. Not everybody wants to know how to make money which is why they outsource this role to somebody else. And, for some people, it makes perfect sense to do that. After all, why would you want to spend years learning a specific skill to become an expert when you can pay a real expert to do it for you at a fraction of the time and cost?

That's why my clients use me and if you have a business it's the same reason that your clients use you. I know that my car mechanic can do a much better job to replace my brakes than I ever could. Similarly, my clients know that I can manage their share portfolios much better than they ever could.

However, learning about money is a very different proposition to learning about fixing a car. Learning about money is a skill that everybody should know. And it's a skill that everybody can learn.

Now you have the DIP, there's no reason why you can't learn this skill for yourself.

CHAPTER 18

IT'S TIME TO MAKE SOME MONEY

THE DIP IS THERE FOR YOU

While it's hard not to feel a little protective over the DIP Strategy, it is ultimately there for everybody to use and enjoy. That must be the way because the concepts and ideas that I am using are already available to everybody. Let's face it, the idea of income-paying shares is not new, and there is nothing revolutionary about trying to pick companies that pay high dividends. That's been going on for a hundred years. So, I can hardly copyright that.

However, I do believe that what I have created in terms of how I have *combined* income and capital growth with capital protection is unique. How I have been able to harness the momentum and volatility of equities to mimic derivatives using the elastic band analogy is something which I have created myself entirely. I have read hundreds of books and not once have I seen this approach to investing.

Does that mean that I am the only person in the world that invests in this way?

I don't think so. I can't believe that I am the only person to have figured something out which is quite simple. Therefore, there may well be some professional traders dotted elsewhere in the world who already follow a very similar approach. If there are, I don't know them and certainly, they don't use the risk variables that I do or the mean risk rating system that I have built. That's all down to me.

Might there be some firms who will take what I have created and put their name to it, yes, I'm sure there will be. And that's okay because I can't stop them. I already knew that risk before I considered writing this book, and it's one of the reasons that I didn't release it earlier. Because I know that some firms and professionals will copy it.

But in any case, I didn't write this book for professional investors, for investment banks, hedge funds, derivatives traders or financial experts.

This book is for you – it's for the average investor who wants more control over their finances and is willing to learn how to do that. I absolutely know that this strategy is unique and that it can help so many people who want to be financially free, not just here in the UK but all over the world.

I say that with confidence because working in the financial world for more than two decades, I have spoken to literally tens of thousands of retail investors. Yes, that's correct, I'm not exaggerating – *tens of thousands* of investors. And I can tell you that not even one of those investors that I have spoken to over the past 25 years has ever told me that they use an investment approach that looks anything like the one that I have created.

Would I have heard of a fund if it was already implementing this strategy? I would have thought so, but that's not to say that some funds aren't already doing something similar. I really don't know, and quite frankly, I'm not sure if I really care.

What I do care about is that the stock market is a behemoth ocean of vast amounts of money just sitting there for individuals smart enough to stake their claim. There is so much money in the stock market that if distributed equally amongst the population we could eradicate world poverty. And the only way to do that is to equip people with the knowledge that they need.

There are millions of investors around the world all doing a very similar thing, the wrong thing, the classic buy and hold game. Sure, it makes them money (some of the time) but that's only because the stock market always goes up in the long term. This doesn't negate the fact that this tired investment approach is wildly inefficient, cost-ineffective and exposes investors to unnecessary risk.

Of course, there are variations to this strategy. For example, some investors might not regard themselves as buy and hold investors because at least once or twice a year they change a few things around in their portfolio just to freshen it up a little. But that's still a buy and hold strategy.

If at the time of purchase, you don't know your precise exact strategy it means that you are almost certainly going to hold that stock for much longer than you should. That's what we humans do. We can't be trusted, myself included.

That's why we need systems in place to take that decision away from us.

Think about it for a moment. What would you call a strategy where an investor buys something and then holds it for quite a long time, at least a few months and possibly even a few years, and whilst doing so ignores all of the company news announcements, the dividend pay-outs, the global market news, the economic data, and even ignores the price of the investment?

And what about the exit strategy for those shares? Are those all-important selling decisions predicated on some fantastic, analytical data that has been researched or is it because the investor wakes up one day and thinks *"the stock market seems to be quite high"* or worse still considers *"I think I might sell. I really could do with a new kitchen"*.

That's the truth, isn't it? Look, I've been there before too, I know how it feels. I was just lucky enough to find an alternative because this is the game that I have dedicated my life to.

The buy and hold myth isn't a genuine strategy, and deep down as intelligent people, we should all be able to see that. We just try and kid ourselves because otherwise, it feels like gambling and nobody wants to think that they're gambling with their life savings. The good intention to do the right thing is always there, to monitor, to analyse, to research, to adapt, to make money – but then the motivation wanes and the strategy, if there ever was one, is out of the window.

That is the truth for 95% of retail investors.

We can all agree that to make money we must abide by the universal principle of <u>buy low and sell high</u> – but then we fail to define what 'low' or 'high' even means.

The *buy low and sell high* mantra has echoed around the financial world for generations and yet very few people attempt to even calculate it - what price is low and what price is high? Even fewer investors are paying attention to the *market momentum* which creates price movement in the first place.

If we don't understand momentum or price action, we have zero chance of being able to accurately define when to buy or sell.

That's why the DIP is so important, it answers one of the most important questions of all - *where* is the market momentum coming from and *why?*

What is driving momentum and how will it impact the price?

You can see the problem. Most private investors just don't know.

And yet everybody, including those who know nothing about investing, knows that a company which pays a high dividend is more attractive than a comparable company for the same amount of risk which pays a lower dividend.

I believe that a dividend is the anchor that so many investors are missing. Using dividends in this way means that finally, we have a starting point to work from, we have a point of reference to make comparisons with. Now we can see how those dividends compare with other forms of returns – interest on savings, the rental yield on properties etc. Most importantly we can use dividends to predict price movement.

For 99% of investors who don't know how to value a company, the price of a stock on its own means absolutely nothing – all share prices on their own mean nothing. We are all assuming that the price must be right because that's the market price. It sounds crazy but that's exactly what we do.

And, so when companies explode into the stratosphere as they did during the dot com bubble, investors assume that the price must be correct without understanding the underlying business. Eventually, the bubble pops and everybody loses everything that they worked for.

Remember that the stock market price that you see is almost always wrong, it's never right. The only time that it is right is when it passes for that very short period of time during the point of equilibrium. That's it. For the rest of the time, it's wrong.

That's why the DIP helps to give clarity on whether a price is too high or too low. It makes sense of the price and it gives it context.

I'm not saying that other strategies don't work. There are many strategies which I am sure work just as well as the DIP, but they involve different elements of the game, speculating, day-trading, penny shares, arbitrage trading, technical analysis, fundamental investing and various other approaches. That's not my game and that's not the conundrum that the DIP is trying to solve. This is all about the income and it's designed for investors who like income.

The problem is that investors who like income have been brain-washed into believing that because they hold dividend-paying shares, they must never sell.

Income is powerful, capital growth is powerful, but the most powerful approach is to combine the two.

Simple concept, beautiful.

HOW MUCH MONEY DO I NEED?

So, let's consider how much money you need to invest to use and make a success of the DIP.

Firstly, I want to tell you that whilst I manage portfolios which range in size considerably, the average portfolio size that I apply the DIP strategy to is a few hundred thousand pounds.

However, that's only because the firm has a minimum portfolio size requirement in order for it to be cost-effective from a business perspective. If you are planning to use the DIP strategy yourself then you don't have that restriction and you could get the same results with a portfolio of just £5,000 or even less.

That's because the cost of dealing is so cheap. There are several online brokers which will allow you to buy and sell shares for just £7. Yes, that's right, £7, the same price as two cups of coffee.

You have to choose a firm where there are no set-up costs, annual fees or ongoing management charges which means that you have complete trading control with absolutely minimal costs. You could even open up a stocks and shares ISA which would mean that all of your profits are tax-free.

If you had a share portfolio of £10,000 you could build a portfolio of 10 DIP companies and scale up the returns relatively quickly. That's the beauty of stock market investing over property investing.

STOCK MARKET V PROPERTY INVESTING

I love the property but over the years and through various unfair tax changes, the Government has made it increasingly difficult for investors to make money. Luckily, at least for now, the Government is making it easy for investors to put their money into the stock market. I suspect it's because the Government is worried that we will all be relying on the state to pay for us in our old age, which is why it encourages us to invest.

In any case, there are many advantages to investing in the stock market over the property market. For a start, you can invest in the stock market with a very small pot of money to begin with, which means no serious significant financial commitment. To buy a house it's the opposite - you need at least a few thousand pounds just to pay for stamp duty, solicitor fees and surveys so straight away you are heavily committed and already in a loss-making position. With trading, however, you have no upfront costs. Every pound that you own can be invested straight into the asset i.e. into the equity. The only cost is the commission (£7) and stamp duty (0.5%) and that's it.

It's also super easy to sell shares if you ever get cold feet. With a click of a button, you can sell your investments and within 2-3 days your money will be sitting back in your bank account. You can't do that with property. It can take months to sell through an estate agent and can cost thousands of pounds. It's completely illiquid.

Then there's the tax to consider. Any money that you make in property is taxable either as income or capital growth, but with stock market ISAs and SIPPs all dividends and capital growth are completely tax-free. In fact, with a SIPP the Government actually *pays you* to invest in it. You even have junior ISAs which are also very tax-efficient and a great product for children and there's also a product called a LISA (Lifetime ISA) which has even greater benefits.

Then there's the management of your share portfolio. You can automate the process which means little time required by you to manage your investments. Property on the other hand usually involves fixing broken-down boilers and painting fences. And if you get a letting agent to do it, that's money coming straight out of your profits so either way, it's going to cost you to manage your buy-to-let portfolio, whether through your wallet or through your time.

There's also the risk to consider.

Tenants can stop paying you rent and can even refuse to leave the property. It can often take many months and tens of thousands of pounds to evict tenants through the court system. You don't have that problem with the stock market. Cash-rich, FTSE100 companies will do everything possible to keep their shareholders happy which means paying dividends and where possible even increasing them. It's like having the best ever tenants, they always pay on time and they never miss a payment.

Other risks are also much lower with the stock market. If you make a mistake and buy a share at a higher price than it's worth or perhaps you just bought a share in a declining sector, the good news is that you can sell it any time and walk away, even if that means selling with a small loss. You can even guarantee the worst-case scenario so that you can restrict the downside with a stop-loss so that you can't lose more than say 10%. This means you can control the maximum fall that you can suffer.

You can't do that with property. If you overpay for your house or you realise after buying the house that you're next to the neighbours from hell, or perhaps there's going to be a motorway built at the end of your garden, well it means that you're stuck. And because of the illiquidity issue, you won't be able to find a buyer very easily which means that you just have to wait and hope for a price recovery.

Finally, the overall control that you have when you invest in the stock market can't be replicated anywhere else, and certainly not with property. There is no other investment opportunity that allows you to make money so quickly and easily if you know what you're doing.

With property, you don't have that safety net. When things go bad, you're stuck with that house.

In my opinion and whilst I love property and think it's a great form of investment, I believe that the stock market wins every time for the reasons I have stated. Of course, once you build your wealth then it will be natural to diversify into new asset classes and there will be a time to invest in property, provided that you know what you're doing.

All of the wealthiest people that I know have 90% or more of their total investable wealth either in the stock market or in a property. This tells you everything that you need to do.

FINANCIAL FREEDOM MEANS CHOICES

Making money is important because it's the only way that allows us to live our lives with freedom of choice. The freedom to do what we want, when we want and with whom we want. The freedom to travel, to have wonderful experiences, the freedom to help our loved ones, or the freedom to help complete strangers and make a difference in the world.

If we all agree that the freedom of choice is something that we should aspire to, then this means one thing – we need to understand the vehicle that will give us that freedom, which is money. Yes, money really does make the world go round.

Understanding money and having a reliable system that generates it for you, is what will give you the freedom of choice in life. Relying only on your work, the state pension, your property portfolio or the local bookies is not the answer.

You need something consistent, something powerful and something which you can control.

ARE YOU READY TO LEARN MORE?

This book was written to show investors how to make money in the stock market in a simple, easy-to-follow and methodical way, and hopefully, I have succeeded in doing that.

However, if you are looking to implement the DIP then you should not regard this as the end of your journey, but rather the beginning. Now is the time to consider whether you want to take the next step and to learn the exact trading strategy.

If you want to learn more, then there's a full online training course which I have created.

I have made the course cost-effective so that anybody can learn. Unfortunately it seems that today the market has become awash with so-called guru traders offering 'the secrets of trading' which are just not true. That's why I feel that I need to do something to change the false narrative.

That's one of the main reasons that I've put this course together; it's to try and counter the noise and harmful information that is out there on the internet. There are very few professional investors like me who teach what they know. I can understand why; it's because they are very comfortable trading for themselves. I used to think like that too but not anymore.

I've got to a stage in my life where money is important, but sharing my knowledge is more important. I feel that I have a duty to shine a light on the one thing that I do know a lot about. As you know I have more than 25 years of trading experience, of which 20 years has been in the City of London, at the very heart of the financial markets. I have worked for some of the biggest investment banks and for some of the smallest brokerage firms and this has allowed me a unique insight into these two warring factions along the way. I have made many mistakes, whilst continuing to develop, learn and improve my varying skill sets across the investment world.

You also know that I still work in the City today and run my own FCA regulated stockbroker business which is responsible for the financial security and well-being of hundreds of clients. In fact, I personally manage investments which run into many tens of millions of pounds for those clients and so I'm held accountable every step of the way, for the wins and the losses.

I tell you this so that you understand why I believe that I am in a great position to help so many people. The course is my way of helping investors, to bypass the false information from imposters masquerading as investment experts so that people can really see what works.

I also wanted to make sure that it wasn't just the rich and successful who were fortunate enough to use my techniques.

Most of my clients are reasonably affluent and so implementing the DIP, along with other strategies allows them to become even more financially secure. That's great for them but I'm also interested in helping the person who doesn't have a lot of money and who doesn't have a substantial share portfolio. My business won't allow me to help them because I just don't have the time to accept smaller accounts. Unfortunately, it's just not viable because I provide bespoke portfolio management to each of my clients.

I don't put client money into funds. I build funds. That takes a lot of time because each fund is unique to the end client, and no two funds are the same. That's why I can't accept accounts below a certain threshold.

But that shouldn't mean that I can't help those who don't have a lot of money. I can still help that new graduate who has just left

University and wants to get into trading or that person who is stuck in a dead-end job and is desperate to find a way out. I can still help the frustrated housewife who has given up her well-paid job to look after the children but feels like she isn't being useful, even though she's doing the most difficult and most important job in the world. I'd like to help the person who is retired and is not happy with how his investments are being managed by his advisor and wants to take back control. I want to help the intrepid traveller who needs money to survive but wants more out of life than just a job and loves to explore continents and embark on incredible adventures. I would love to help the people who are in poorer parts of the world and who feel trapped because they can't see a way out.

The great thing with trading is that it's open to everybody; you just need a computer and an internet connection.

With this book, hopefully, I can help a lot of people.

For those of you who want to know more about the DIP or just want to watch and learn from the free training modules, just visit www.dividendincomeplus.co.uk or email info@dividendincomeplus.co.uk

THANK YOU, AND GOOD LUCK

That's it, guys and girls. Thank you for joining me on this epic journey. If I have been able to help you in any way, then I'm glad that I was able to and I hope that what you have learned makes a real difference in your life. I really mean that.

If I have been able to show you something in this book that will improve your standard of living, which will help you to achieve a better life on your terms which means better choices for you and your family, that would really mean the world to me. I'm a Sikh and in my faith to help others should be a part of my spiritual path. If I am able to help a complete stranger to achieve even some of their financial goals and dreams that would mean a huge thing to me. In fact, it would be one of my greatest achievements.

I would love you to share your success stories with me in a few years' time and let me know whether I was able to make a difference.

Hopefully, there are things that I have written in this book which will really resonate with you, which will make you think differently for the first time in your life about what is truly possible.

And remember that this book is not about me, it's not about the stock market, and despite its title, it's not even about the DIP Strategy.

This book is actually all about *you*. It's about what you are capable of achieving with the right mindset and approach. That's why the DIP strategy doesn't belong to me.

It's yours, it belongs to everybody who needs it and wants to use it.

I will leave you with this final thought.

I am very proud to say that I came from a very humble background, the youngest of four children growing up in a poor, working-class family in Coventry. My parents were not educated, in fact, the exact opposite. They could barely speak English as they came into this country as immigrants from Panjab in search of a better life in the 1960s. They worked incredibly hard and sacrificed so much to give me an opportunity in life. I took that opportunity and in so doing have changed my life and the lives of several members of my family forever.

I have also had the opportunity to help change the lives of underprivileged families that I barely knew and who have now become good friends.

The point is that money is an incredible weapon that can be used to help heal the world, to help put food on somebody's table or to help a poor child receive an education so they have a chance to live a better life.

By most people's definition, at least in terms of financial freedom, you could say that I 'made it', whatever 'made it' is supposed to mean. I'm not sure if I agree with that statement but if I did make it, then I know that you can make it too. The game of finance is an easy one to play and an even easier one to win once you understand the rules.

This is a real chance for you to help your family become more financially secure and give them a better and brighter future through the freedom of choice.

I am sincerely grateful to you for spending the time that you have with me. From the bottom of my heart, thank you.

Finally, and whilst I have been careful not to make any promises in this book, I will break my golden rule on this one occasion and leave you with my personal guarantee...

...Investing in the Stock Market really shouldn't be difficult.

"The DIP is brilliant. My advisors have been using it for about two years and so far, I've been very impressed with the results."

W HADLEY, ST IVES

"I have definitely made significantly more money in buying and selling Aviva than I ever would have made by just holding it."

D WARDLAW, CUMBRIA

"I have been investing in the stock market for several decades but the DIP is definitely one the best strategies that I have come across."

M CROCKER, CUMBRIA

"I invested using the DIP strategy in 3 FTSE100 companies and in less than 2 months I made on average 73% in profit plus dividends."

K HANSON, TODMORDEN

"I was previously following a different investment strategy which was not doing that well. Then I was introduced to the Dividend Income Plus Strategy by my advisors and in less than four months it has completely transformed things.

If the performance continues like this I am seriously going to consider transferring the Halifax Stocks and Shares ISAS for me and my wife"

J BLACKBURN, CAMBRIDGE

"My portfolio has improved the most with the new dividend strategy. In 6 months the DIP made 29% in Centamin, 20% in Burberry and 17% in Bodycote, results that I am very pleased with. MAN Group has proven my 'worst' performer so far but it's still up a creditable 3%"

R BROOKS, NEWQUAY

Ranjeet Singh is a London-based stockbroker with over two decades-worth of experience managing and growing stock portfolios in the UK and global equities markets. The youngest of four children, Ranjeet was born to immigrant parents who came to the UK in search of a better life in the early 1960s.

After graduating with an MSc in Business Economics from Brunel University, he began his working career at Lloyds Bank before eventually moving his way up to Deutsche Bank.

In 2008, at the height of the financial crash, he founded the FCA-regulated stock broking firm London Stone Securities, which he still leads today, helping his clients to invest safely and securely.

In his personal life, Ranjeet is the founder and trustee of a UK based charity to help eradicate hate crimes and is involved in numerous endeavours to help the financially disadvantaged as well as victims of racial abuse. He is also a keen writer and an author of five children's books. He has travelled to many remote places around the world in search of adventure, including camping in the Mongolian desert, travelling on the Tran-Siberian railway, and trekking through Colombian rainforests. Closer to home he is a keen Krav Maga martial artist and a big fan of Liverpool football club.

Just in case things aren't busy enough for him, Ranjeet has followed in his parents' footsteps and is the proud father of four young children: Gioia, Giorgia, Fateh Singh and Himmat Singh.

Printed in Great Britain
by Amazon

38626027R00134